FUNNY
BUSINESS

MANAGEMENT
UNMASKED

RODNEY MARKS, BENJAMIN MARKS
AND ROBERT SPILLANE

SECOND EDITION: COMPLETELY
DEVISED AND OUTDATED

GOKO PUBLISHING

To learn more about GOKO Publishing you can visit us at:
www.GOKOPublishing.com

Second edition, 2017, © Rodney Marks,
Benjamin Marks, Robert Spillane
First published in Australia, 2006, as
The Management Contradictionary
by Michelle Anderson Publishing, Melbourne

Funny Business: Management Unmasked

GOKO Management and Publishing
PO Box 7109
McMahons Point 2060
Sydney. Australia

Library of Congress Cataloging-in-Publication data

**Marks, Rodney; Marks Benjamin; Spillane, Robert
Funny Business: Management Unmasked
p. cm.
ISBN-13: 9781613399149
LCCN: 2017908670**

**To contact the publisher please
email info@GOKO.com.au**

10 9 8 7 6 5 4 3 2

'Don't judge a book by its cover.'
Page Turner, *Aphorists' Pundit*

'Thanks for the review copy. I got my
money's worth, that's for sure.'
Lex Icon, Times Literary Supplement, London

'Please wait. Your call is important to us.'
Eddie Torriolle (voicemail), New
York Times Review of Books

'If I was interested in management terms and knew
how to read, this is without a doubt the book I would
buy. Highly recommended: ***** (five stars).'
Harry Diculous, leadership visionary

'Exhaustive but not tiring, blunt yet refined, sharp
yet touchy, comprehensive yet comprehensible, simple
but not simplistic, timely yet ageless, funny yet serious,
understandable yet learned, amazing but not corny.'
Haydn de Mudd, corporate governance authority

'The authors are on-song yet unsung.'
Perry Pheral, business ethicist

'A must read! Please send me a copy, or an original.'
Noel Hedge, Hon. PhD

'I've never had so much fun under the
covers and between the sheets.'
Candida Cockburn, work-life balance expert

Dedications

To my parents, Kevin and Marcelle: **RM**

To RM and RS: **BM**

To BM and RM: **RS**

Disclaimer

It's not our fault.

Acknowledgements

The Devil made us do it.

ability

The capacity to prove potential capability. The attribute that distinguishes competent managers from incontinent ones. Diminutive for billability.

abnormal

Not like me. Common reasons for frequenting the gym.

about-face

A 180 degree policy reversal. Often revolutionary; that is, 360 degrees; also known as an O-curve. An about-face is usually prefaced by denial, a refusal to apologise and an appeal to pragmatism. Anything after a preface.

above-the-line

Paid promotion that you agree is a gamble, such as TV, radio and print advertising. Expenses worth underlining.

absenteeism

(See **presenteeism***)*

absurdity

A belief said to be false by someone, like me, who does not share it.

academia

Hard-shelled nuts.

academic

The most insulting word in any language.

accident

Lack of belief in predetermination or the divine providence of coincidence. Unbudgeted research. Or what should have been within room for error.

account executive

Semi-permeable listening device.

accountability

An out-of-fashion concept that refers to people being held responsible for their own actions. Pre-dates, and made redundant by, the concept of blaming, which is central to organisational behaviour.

accounting

The rewriting of history, in columns and rows, to justify to shareholders what you did with their money. Counting.

accounts payable

Money you'll eventually pay those suppliers who you've selected to keep in business.

accounts receivable

Money that's owed to you by customers using you as their choice of bank, due to your preferred terms: no loan application fee, no interest, no credit rating downgrade. Best located in the marketing department.

acccuracy

Presicely. Claims that will haunt you.

achievement

Abandoning a larger task.

acquisition

(See **merger***)*

acronyms and initialisms

Short-cuts to obscurity.

action

A delegated task.

actionable

Any task delegated to someone else.

activism

The belief that campaigning to bring about political or social change will bring about political or social change. And the belief that the change will last and be worthwhile.

actors

Managers: those who strut and fret their hour upon the stage, then are heard no more.

actuary

Someone who tells your insurer when you should die. The reason for separation of powers

added value

Something substituted for deducted value.

adhocracy

Any organisational unit other than your own.

adjacencies

Positive spin on mission creep.

administrivia

A management task imposed on you.

advertisement

1. An untruth tolerated as entertainment. Or true words accompanying false pictures.

2. A glowing endorsement organised and paid for by the endorsee.

advertising

Creating demand for something by highlighting its worst feature.

advertising standards

The ethical benchmarking of paid public persuasion.

advisory panel

A pane in the glass.

affairs

Intra-corporate entrepreneurship.

affiliate

1. *(noun)* A person or organisation with a hierarchical ranking somewhere between an associate and a partner

2. *(verb)* *T*o align your values with another's by disregarding any that are not shared.

affirmative action

Discrimination against the successful. Coercion in the name of equality. Choosing equality over quality.

affluence

Your personal assistant has a PA.

after-sales service

Mythical organisational process, sometimes located in an imaginary, eponymous department with a toll-free number.

ageism

The belief that all ages are the same – even in their differences.

agenda

Secret list of outcomes unknown to all meeting participants.

agent

A commissioned friend.

aggression

Part of the managerial power game, compensating for a lack of technical expertise.

AGM (Annual General Meeting)

Yearly public book-ending of apology and astrology, where top management attest they have read what they signed.

agreement

Reluctant, begrudging, antipathetic acceptance.

aim

Off-target archery metaphor, whose misguided objectives are to add more strings to the bow of direction, and to insert more arrows in the quiver of purpose.

alcohol

Liquid in which to dissolve business ethics. Helps prevent managerialese.

alcoholism

Shot of holism imbibed by managers.

alienation

What successful managers feel.

alignment

An agreeable truce, based on battle exhaustion, when ADHD has become PTSD.

alliance

A union of managers who lie to others to such an extent that they cannot decide how to lie to their deserving superiors.

all things being equal *(ceteris paribus)*

Taking variables away.

all your ducks are in a row

As in 'all your stars are aligned', this business cliché refers to a series of chance events which serendipitously support your argument, strategy or business.

alliance

Working together under your direction.

allocation

Notionally an economic term about choosing where to distribute resources over time. It is the real exercise of power, being the manifestation of favouritism, cronyism, nepotism and incompetence, which economists generally illustrate rather than explain.

alternative

Going out on a limb (i.e., on the other hand) or a whim.

altruism

Helping others for your own satisfaction. The umbrella term for all isms.

ambition

Point of difference in career advancement when your achievements are not enough. When your aims speak louder than your actions.

analogy

Something you catch from cross-pollinated ideas.

analysis

Being anal about the banal.

(*See* **ballpark**)

analysis paralysis

Assessing a project initially qualitatively and ultimately quantitatively against a plethora of hierarchies and an aggregation of continua followed by a collection of assessment criteria before feeding the raw data back into the system and up the line with a request for further funding.

analytical

A qualifier used to mask gut-feel.

antique

The antics of a superannuated leader. Anything not updated within the past three years.

antitrust legislation

Proof of government distrust of business. Enforced by government monopolies.

Thought: If government represents business, but business does not represent government, on what basis is antitrust legislation good and tax evasion bad?

anxiety

Worry brought on by managers contemplating the legitimacy of their profession.

anziety

1. The stress felt by a manager after sending an email to the team leader, prior to spell-checking.

2. Anxiety Down Under.

apology

Preparing the ground for a future indiscretion. Usually preceded by a denial.

appeal

1. A cry in the wilderness.

2. A clarion call.

application

Pathetic attempt to fit your background into the selection criteria by writing a self-referential reference.

(*See* **résumé**)

appointment

Pointed reference to a placement in which you no longer control your diary.

appraise

To report on what you feel before the facts are reality tested.

apprentice

A PA with ambition.

aptitude test

Battery of circuitous quizzes designed to assess your endurance, your positives and negatives, and the calibre of your weaponry.

argh

Onomatopoeic sound that computer gurus make when they discover that they aren't. It means 'argh'.

argument

Argued against.

Arial

This is a clear font unencumbered by curly bits and is the style choice for emails. When being clear it is crucial to say that you are being clear, even if you have several hidden agendas. By merely saying that something is in *Arial* your audience will suspend disbelief, even if it is in *Times New Roman*.

aristocrats

People who know they are the best, contrasted with managers, who know they aren't.

arts, the

When presenting as cultured and part of the culture, the arts are worth sponsoring for networking over nibbles.

assembly line

A sequenced method of manufacturing robots from humans.

assessment centre

1. An administration established to milk the belief that psychologists understand behaviour

2. A place that unfairly benefits those who look the same.

assets

1. Necessary counterweight for balanced accounts, and accountants

2. Temporarily valued budget items available to support the career advancement of senior and chief executives

3. Optimism quantified

4. Liabilities waiting to happen.

assumption

Well, you have to start somewhere.

attendance

What you're paid for. A measure used by those who believe in the labour theory of value.

attitude

Mythical entity used by managers to manipulate high performers. Can be singular or plural, but out of many comes one, which in other contexts is quite a good motto.

audit

A waste of time only the paranoid prepare for – and they're right.

auditorium

A place to audit.

auditor

1. Someone who puts glasses on their ears

2. A heartless ticker whose role it is to add green or purple to black and red

3. A hard of hearing earwig who wants a hearing

4. An impurist who mistakes finance for mathematics.

authoritarian

Directive management style, in which the leader leads.

authority

1. Those in a state of needless leaderlessness, as there is no-one higher to refer to

2. A fictitious quality of managers, by which power over others can be enforced.

autocrat

A manager who gets things done, even if the organisation is destroyed in the process.

automation

The recognition that because subordinates are automatons, we may as well have robots doing the work.

autonomy

The authority, in the afterlife, to work independently.

average

1. Means mean

2. A safe place for managers to be

3. Dividing the sum of the whole by the number of its parts will yield the average, but will not show how the sum of the whole can be greater than the whole when reconstituted. Translated into management terms, a group made up of people with average ability will only ever be average.

back-of-the-envelope calculation

A handwritten recommendation, short on research, rationale, comparisons of alternatives, consultation, planning, number-crunching, data-mining and theory, which often represents a better option.

backgrounding

History of the idea of the theoretical premise of the day.

bad debt

Debt that hasn't been paid yet.

bads

Unwanted goods, like and including government services, because they have no (voluntary) customers.

ballpark

Close enough to be acceptable to you.

balls

Needed to be grasped by female managers to control pricks.

bandit

(*See* **banker**)

bank

Den of inequity in which you lose interest through buying money. Place where savings means loans.

banker

(*See* **bandit**)

bankrupt

The inability to pay for past losses with future cash.

basic

An entry level standard that can be used as the benchmark for charging more for an acceptable model.

bear market

Environment in which shares are traded on the basis of share-traders not believing the bull received from companies. A soft furry big scary market.

behaviour

What you do before you're caught at it.

behavioural science

(*See* **misbehavioural science**)

behaviourism

In managerial psychology, the view that the mind studies mindless behavior. The brainchild of a group of American psychologists whose disbelief in the human psyche led them to worship dogs, rats and pigeons.

below-the-line

Paid and unpaid promotion over which you pretend to have control, such as PR, in-store offers and direct selling.

benchmark

The quality standard that you can get away with.

benchmarking

An arbitrary standard, without a bench or marking.

benefit

Something believed to be more valuable than the cost.

best practice

1. The quality standard to refer to when you've been caught out merely benchmarking

2. The standard asserted when it's not self-evident.

(*See* **benchmark** *and* **benchmarking**)

bias

1. Rolling towards my centre and away from yours

2. Employing a prostitute.

big business

1. An allusion to the fallacy that all large corporations have aligned financial interests and shared views on public policy

2. A small business that has lost its way.

(*See* **small business**)

big picture

A larger frame to refer to if the data do not support your vision.

bill

1. Invoicing process, especially useful to expedite in advance, as in the accountants' triple mantra:

   - bill early, pay late;

   - buy low, sell high; and

   - cash is king

2. Gentle reminder by a supplier about money that they believe you might owe them.

blue-collar

The uniform of the working class, worn so that they will not be inadvertently distracted from making and fixing stuff by being asked to fill in forms, such as tax invoices or receipts.

board of directors

Group of mainly men who went to the same private school last millennium, have shared values and world views, and can easily substitute for each other should golf or sailing or overseas holidays or divorce proceedings interfere with attendance at meetings.

body language

The discourse of dubious, doubtful descriptions posturing as science, and the body of attitudes gesturing towards meaningful symbols.

bold

1. What fortune favours: making a fortune out of favouritism

2. Somewhere between CAPITALISATION and *italicisation* in the continuum of screaming messages.

bonus

1. Salary that you have to work for

2. Salary that you have to retire for.

book

1. Bound text-and-paper compilation used as reading material before being replaced by film, television and the Internet

2. Portable graffiti

3. Educational instrument unfamiliar to managers

4. Place to hide confidential information

5. Interim summary of work-in-progress.

(*See* **The Book**, *which is something to throw at disruptors, to no effect*)

bookish

1. Manager bound up in his words
2. Manager bound by his words
3. Someone so awkward that they want to be seen to be reading or to have read.

boom-bust cycle

Standard justification for doing badly after doing well.

bore

A manager who talks when he should listen – and when he listens, still talks.

boredom

Rule by a bore.

borrow

To obtain money or something else of value (such as a cup of sugar or a lawnmower) by saying that it will be paid back sometime, often with interest in the form of more money, sugar or grass clippings.

bottom line

The only real way to find out what actually happens. Looking down to see if it is okay to look up.

brainstorming

1. Lightning rod for a team thundering under the effects of electroshock therapy

2. Clouding the mind.

brand

Emblem, symbol, icon or wording that assists consumers and potential consumers to ignore intrinsic merits or lack thereof.

brand awareness

1. Making awareness a brand attribute

2. Making a new brand brand new

3. Making an old brand brand new

4. People knowing the above.

brand loyalty

1. Loyalty irrespective of reciprocity

2. What producers demand of consumers when features and benefits are not persuasive.

break-even point

The point on the timeline of a project's lifecycle where it stops haemorrhaging money.

bribery

Incentive payment.

briefing

Pre-preparing by backgrounding.

broker of hope

Pawning IQ for EQ.

BS

1. Business School
2. Bible Study
3. Bloated Syntax
4. Business Spin
5. CEO-speak
6. doublespeak
7. doubletalk
8. government policies
9. corporate policies
10. election promises
11. parliamentary preambles
12. political core and non-core promises
13. annual reports

14. start-ups' pitch documents

15. social entrepreneurs' claims

16. secular ethics centres' preaching

17. religions' promises of immortality

18. a nonsensical and subliminal postscript (PS) in a snail mail letter or an email, whereby the PS is the whole point of the message of the missive.

(*See* **bullshit**)

budget

A fable chronicled in columns and rows, without a moral.

budget allocation

What you spend as leverage for more.

built-to-last

A product that will work perfectly well until you're promoted.

bull market

Environment in which shares are traded on the basis of bull received from companies.

bullshit

1. What stops managers killing each other

2. Managing Directors' advice to their own remuneration subcommittees.

(*See* **BS**)

bureaucracy

Multi-layered black hole into which people, physical resources, money and time are sucked, never to reappear.

bureaucrat

A crat who has fallen from the mantle onto the bureau.

business cycle

Not what it used to be, and never was. Neither caused by business nor a cycle. Are money supply and interest rates government controlled?

business ethics

1. All manner of good and bad things as good and bad, but not necessarily in that order

2. Moving set of temporary values created by organisations to quash uninformed criticism from government and shareholders.

business expenses

1. Items successfully claimed as tax deductions
2. Items bought with government money for private benefit.

business lunch

1. A way to accumulate frequent intake incentives
2. A way to accumulate frequent imbibe brownie points
3. A method to benefit from feeding and watering the cattle class
4. Putting the quid into quid pro quo
5. A bribe
6. Positive reinforcement
7. A bargaining chip for extortion
8. A bargaining chip for blackmail
9. A bonus
10. A carrot to an individual in order to stick it to a group
11. Wholesaling retail influence peddling
12. Extraction of personal gratification from professional negotiations
13. Intimacy with legitimacy
14. Precursor to a post-prandial nap

15. Precursor to cursing.

business model

A reverse-engineered retrofitted abstraction of reality, accurate after the fact, because of the fact.

business objective

The second part of the two-part ubiquitous training program, 'Business Aims and Objectives', which has no relationship to what executives think about, talk about or actually do.

business park

1. A campus whose premises are based on assumptions

2. An oxymoron, like fun run, petty cash, spend thrift, job security, crisis management and home office.

business plan

Hypothetical and theoretical, tentative and hesitant pathway to the future, measured in various time periods, although no-one has ever seen a five-year plan in its fifth year.

buying-in

The psychological process of requiring employees to agree with bosses.

buzzword

An enthusiastically ambiguous expression used to assert the status of the speaker whilst promising nothing.

(See above and below)

buzzword bingo

How it works –

You don't need an MBA to play a bigger game. Here's a collection keywords, weasel words and buzzwords to help you on your way. Play buzzword bingo with these compost heaps of clear gibberish, garbled gobbledygook and today's clichés from the fantasy worlds of strategy, management and leadership.

Buzzword bingo can be played in several different ways. Start with an empty matrix, a grid or a table, like the one here:

Choose a theme, like marketing, or the AGM, the weekly briefing, and write in on the top of the page. Prior to a meeting, co-create a list of, say, 25 words and phrases that are likely to be overused at that event. Populate the empty template, as in the examples below.

Decide what type of game you wish play. A game may be won by hearing words in a horizontal, vertical or diagonal line, or by marking off all 25 terms. Then, during the meeting, when you hear one buzzword too many, shout 'Bingo!' and go home.

Computing/IT				
bandwidth	googling	program-ming	click-thru	hardware
real time	compatible	inexpensive	scalable	defenestra-tion
Infonesia	seamless	enterprise	keystroke	synchro-nised
error-free	mobility	text-based	expert	Nerdistan
turnkey	next generation	parallel	user-friendly	cloud

Human Resources				
caring	glass ceiling	rotation	challenges	incentivise
satisfaction	climate	indicators	silver ceiling	commit-ment
learning	strengths	competence	motivation	threats
culture	opportuni-ties	transforma-tion	enlarge-ment	perfor-mance
upskilling	enrichment	reskilling	weaknesses	redeploy-ment

Insolvency				
acquisition	exit strategy	negative growth	succession plan	Chapter 11
exposure	negative profit	circling the drain	fire sale	optimism
contingency	broker and broker	outplace	debt recovery	legacy firm
release people	down the tubes	let go	rightsizing	endgame
liquidation	the way forward	exit interview	merger	transitioning

Leadership				
adhocracy	empty suit	mindset	chaos	excellence
organisation	Collaboration	fast track	rankism	consultation
functional	Reinvention	continuous	herding cats	responsive
dialogue	Integrated	robust	direction	knowledge
stress	Discourse	leverage	thought	followership

Management				
benchmark	efficient	infrastructure	best practice	empowerment
insourcing	capability	environment	matrix	catalyst
feedback	megadigm	change	flexibility	model
dotted line	granularity	multimedia	downsizing	heads up
next level	effective	high quality	offline	middle office

Administration

offshoring	proactive	silos	onshoring	responsibility
templatised	org. chart	results-driven	traction	org. tree
rightsizing	transparency	outsourcing	schadenfreude	values
paradigm	scoping	vision	presenteeism	self-managed
win-win	preward	shift	world class	hospital pass

Sales & Marketing

administrivia	high-impact	mindshare	bio break	high-yield
preferred	brandalism	hot-desking	pseudo	cannibalise
ideation	street cred	channelibalise	infotainment	the market
client-centric	leading edge	user-centric	customer	long-term
value-added	cutting edge	low-risk	world first	focus group

Operations

actionable	decision	plan b	activity	disambiguate
post mortem	ballpark	drill down	problematic	built-to-last
guesstimate	queuing	critical	just-in-time	roll out
cycle	metadata	scope creep	data dump	meta-decision

subject creep	obsoles- cence	value chain	data mining	production

Strategy				
alliance	fit	partnering	big picture	game plan
re-purpos- ing	reduction	game theory	visioning	intelligence
fad	value stream	war story	ethics	synergy
high-level	thought leader	entry level	strategic	governance
caveat	restructur- ing	gap analysis	case study	war story

Weasel words				
behaviours	ellipsis…	mother- hood	CEO-speak	embedment
non-concur	cliche'	flagpole	obfuscate	cold-call
hybrid	prebuttal	demystifi- cation	impactful	premumble
diplospeak	jargon	psycho- babble	double talk	journalese
xenophobia	alternative truth	eclectic	meander- thal	trial balloon

Acronyms & Initialisms				
1:1	B2G	KPI	24/7	CEO
MBO	80:20	CIO	MBWA	B2A
COO	PICNIC	B2B	CRM	ROA
B2B2C	CYA	ROI	B2C	FAQ
TQM	B2E	GIGO	USP	MBFA

by-product

1. Something tangential that might come out of your core business process; especially useful if that process is a dud

2. The subtext of advertisers' calls-to-action

call centre

The home of highly skilled, headset-wearing, omniscient, omnipresent, omnipotent, polyglot human knowledge repositories with nice telephone manners, condescended to by tomorrow's dole recipients.

calling

Delusion.

candid

Unprepared.

can-do

Present tense of candid.

capital

1. What you had before you allocated it

2. The city where your profit went to.

capitals

A type of impoliteness, YELLING at the reader. Not a capital idea.

career

A life sentence for committing the crime of having a family.

caring

Making loving, giving and sharing believable.

case study

Business war story chosen to support your management philosophy.

cash flow

Key economic indicator of viability. Like sex appeal, you've either got or you haven't, and if you haven't, claims about potential won't help.

cash incentive

Cash.

casualise

1. The professional inability to commit

2. Making staff unemployed at the end of every shift

3. Making staff fight for every session

4. Making overtime over time

5. The belief in the short-term

6. Workplace dating

7. The paradoxical relationship between casual and causal.

catalyst

Someone who causes change in others whilst remaining completely unaffected.

catharsis

Emotional chunder.

caveat

A warning about a warning that lets you off the hook. In fact, if what has been warned about eventuates, even though it might be your fault, both preparedness and prophecy can be claimed by the caveat communicator.

caveat emptor

Let the buyer beware of the seller, because the seller is untrustworthy, unscrupulous, completely devoid of business ethics and likely to defraud; does not apply when you are the seller. Placing the words 'caveat emptor: conditions apply' on all products might prevent litigation.

celebrate

To make someone famous for a moment, merely for doing their job.

celebrity

Prophet in a financial year.

censoring

Filleting your truth for mine, for your own good.

centralisation

1. One end of the autonomy-control continuum, popular when independence fails

2. Using circular reasoning instead of business planning

3. Being diametrically opposed to diameters.

CEO

1. Chief Expert Obfuscator
2. Code Enforcement Officer
3. Chief Entertainment Officer
4. Casualty Evacuation Officer
5. Combine Expensive Operations
6. Catholic Education Office.

CFO

1. Manager who stops the buck
2. Manager who wears a check shirt so that, if the spreadsheet software crashes, it can be pinned to the wall with all those columns and rows adding up to the total in the bottom right-hand cell
3. Manager who ensures that the profit equals the loss.

chair

Manager who tables emotions, and then tabulates them.

chairperson

The individual responsible for casting the seating around the board table and for couching dissent as consensus.

challenges

Problems.

change agent

Someone perennially dissatisfied with their lot – and yours.

change management

Fallacious belief that people want to change their work behaviour or that, even if they want to, they can. A popular way to implement a change management program is to change management.

chaos

What will result if you don't do it my way.

character

Moral fibre lubricating the organisational irritable bowel syndrome of balanced decision-makers. To say a manager has a good character is like saying that an unattractive teenager has a good personality.

charisma

Gift of grace: possessed by miracle-workers who generally die young. Misapplied to managers and politicians.

chauvinism

The defence of management by managers for security.

cheating

1. Disagreement over rules

2. Success by any means

3. A recognition that endemic rule-breaking is central to organisational survival.

children

1. Liabilities

2. Expensive and unreliable couriers for passing messages between former spouses

3. After-hours mistakes

4. Risky investments with a very long pay-off period, or maybe none at all. Not for the faint-hearted.

choice

1. Used by managers to abrogate responsibility

2. What people select to deny that they have options.

circular

(noun) A circumlocutory memo sent on a circuitous route in a roundabout manner.

circular reasoning

(See **reasoning, circular***)*

civilisation

The concealment of avarice with jealousy. Belief in the merit of saving and planning for the future.

clarity

Management communication created under the influence of claret.

classics

1. Your most recent corporate annual report update, memo, proposal, performance evaluation and job application

2. Writings of management gurus, now remaindered, published before you were a manager, containing the collective fads of a fashionable profession.

cleaners

- Employees who work without making a mess

- Employees who make work of mess, as distinct from other employees – who make a mess of work.

cliché

1. Anything following and including the disclaimer: 'I know that this is a cliché, but… '

2. In a nutshell, to get to the root of the matter, at this point in time, it is jargon used by someone else to get more bang for their buck

3. Jargon used by someone else

4. Anyhting French.

client

1. Moral blackmailer

2. Emotional blackmailer

3. Someone who requires work from you

4. Annoying, intrusive individual or organisation who or which regularly makes unreasonable claims on organisational resources, including (but not limited to) requests for products and services paid for, but not received, or if

received, received in a condition inferior to that originally agreed to.

climate change

When culture change fails, and change management doesn't work, contemporary business leaders use climate change to deflect analysis and criticism of internal organisational issues, in much the same way that government leaders use war, poverty, refugees, Third World debt and – climate change.

CLM

1. Career Limiting Move
2. Customer Lifecycle Management
3. Closed Loop Marketing
4. Called, Left Message
5. Continuous Learning Module
6. Common Law Marriage
7. Critical thinking
8. Thought leadership
9. Insubordination
10. Resignation.

club

Tribal meeting place where non-members are beaten about the head.

coach

1. Out-sorcerer of a manager's psyche

2. Someone who assists a manager in the dereliction of his duty to delegate one of the few non-delegatable tasks in his job description

3. Management consultant who improves organisations person by person, and charges accordingly.

coercion

Persuasion by your manager. Caution plus collaboration.

cognitive intelligence

The ability to conceptualise a profit when one doesn't exist, in the face of the facts being drawn to your attention by the clearly unintelligent.

cold call

Asking people you don't know for work, on the basis that people who do know you don't want to work with you. Any call with a hotline at the other end.

collaboration

You doing what I tell you to do, in a timely fashion.

colleague

A competitor known to you by his first name, often working in your organisation and vying with you for promotion and other perks.

collusion

An off-the-record deal, the unremarkable lifeblood of competitive behaviour, which inconveniently becomes public knowledge.

comfort zone

Cosy corner from which managers are required to proactively move forward by thinking laterally, innovatively and creatively, outside the nine dots and beyond the circle.

commerce

Horse-trading by the top end of town.

commitment

Evidence of managerial madness manifested as consent to accountability; punished by being straight-jacketed in a bureaucracy until cured by a dose of lucidity.

committee

A group of expendable employees whose role is to act as a collective scapegoat.

communication

Me telling you.

community

Chance to get away from yourself.

company car

A vehicle for minimising personal income tax whilst transporting you to another place.

(*See* **salary packaging**)

company photo day

If you need a photo to remember something, then it's not worth remembering.

compensation

Inadequate recompense for your time.

competence

Getting away with it.

competitor

Someone whose funeral you're prepared to attend, and even arrange.

computer

1. A device to increase paperwork

2. A machine that timelines the ignorance of IT companies, and is three months out of date as soon as it hits your desk.

computer program

An escalating game played between program developers and program consumers, in which the latter test-market the product at their own expense, making suggestions for improvements that should have been built into the software in the first place.

conditioning

It's not my fault; society is to blame.

conference

An expensive meeting at which people confer.

conflict

1. Two or more individuals or groups of individuals or entities in neither total agreement nor total disagreement over one or more matters of greater or lesser importance in and of themselves

2. Two or more individuals or groups of individuals or entities in total agreement or total disagreement over one or more matters of greater or lesser importance in and of themselves.

conformity

When everyone sings the company song from the same page of the corporate hymn sheet, when all the ducks are in a row, and when the troops – in formation, FYI – line up to salute the company logo.

conglomerate

An organisation so diverse that even it doesn't know what business it is in.

congress

A digressed conference.

conscience

A quality claimed by compliance managers to justify their salaries.

consciousness

1. I

2. That which humans use to deny I.

consensus

Anything preceding a full stop.

conservative

Someone who prefers the jam we're in.

conspiracy

Working together.

consultation

Using *groupthink* to allocate blame.

consumer

1. An anonymous customer

2. An individual who, when aggregated into the

general population mass, becomes responsible for buying everything

3. The boss

4. An all-consuming client.

consumerism

An ism that you can buy into.

consumption

What should happen to production.

contemplation

We're still thinking about this.

contra deal

Bartering to evade tax and other transaction costs.

contradictionary

1. Adding definite meaning to words

2. A dictionary with an annotated self-referential index in the back

3. Numerous defining moments, alphabetised

4. This joke book.

control

(verb) To exercise power over people or organisations who agree to be subjugated.

(noun) Those organisational functions that tell you what happens when.

convention

A convened meeting in which participants pretend to be in a convent.

convergence

The coming together of resources such as people or technology or ideas - yes, intellectual capital is a resource – so that they are no longer parallel, in metaphorical silos or drainpipes, nor are they moving apart. Convergence is more serendipitous than the result of change management processes, consultancies, or leadership.

conversation

Murdered by postmodernists.

cooperation

(*See* **conspiracy**)

coordinate

To administer chaos in a focused way.

copyright

The right to copy.

core

The part of the business you shouldn't eat.

core values

1. Values that must be adhered to, compared with non-sticky values in the values statement

2. Values worth laminating.

corporate comedy

1. Corporate

2. The twenty-first-century equivalent to the court jester: the only person allowed to tell the truth to the modern day feudal lord, namely, the CEO.

corporate communication

Messianic messaging process whereby the views of the corporate godhead are evangelised to the unfaithful at the acolytes' expense.

corporate culture

That unchangeable, intangible organisational feel, the result of history, people, objectives and production, which must be denigrated and decimated by an organisation's leadership if they are to get anything done.

corporate governance

A useful and focused way to blame the board of directors for management mistakes. Much discussed when companies fail; something to do with people who are meant to reign in out-of-control CEOs, except when those executives are doing well and not getting caught.

corporate language

(*See* **buzz words**, **jargon** and **weasel words**)

corporate social responsibility

1. Insurance against unknown future risks, paid by corporations to the broader community, so that an adverse impact upon any section of society can be reduced due to a base level of goodwill towards the firm

2. Supplementary subliminal advertising to groups sceptical – or even *skeptical* – of the spell of mainstream media

(*See* **philanthropy**)

corporation

An amoral, unelected entity, accountable to changing and changeable stakeholders, whose aim is to maximise shareholder value at all costs. And that's why they're so valuable to society.

cost

A truth that hurts.

cost accountant

A reverse prophet.

cost-benefit analysis

The cost of analysing benefits divided by the benefits of analysing costs.

cost centre

Any strategic organisational unit not directly involved in bottom-line activities; all are expendable.

cost effectiveness

A feeble attempt to justify poor purchasing decisions on the basis that the benefits will be seen down the track.

cost of capital

The real price of money.

counselling

The selling and buying of unwanted advice.

coward

1. A manager who sabotages performance with personality

2. A polite leader.

(*See* **moral courage**)

crackdown

This time I mean it.

creativity

1. The ability to think outside the square

2. The ability to think inside the square when everyone is telling you to think outside it

3. The capacity to invent the square

4. The propensity to play with the sides of the square, thereby eliminating its squareness

5. An obsession with all sorts of quasi-geometric iterations while avoiding work

6. Taking credit for the work of others.

credit

Money available to spend, which if you had it you wouldn't, because when you did you did, and you don't want to go down that path again.

crisis

An insufficiency of excuses.

crisis management

Management.

critic

1. Stakeholder
2. Shareholder
3. Opinion holder
4. Funded retiree
5. Politician, especially at election time.

critical path analysis

Like those who sloppily use the terms 'strategy' and 'tactics', adherents to this way of constructing services and products are captured by the metaphor of 'business is war', and think that the manufacture of a can of baked beans is similar to building a Polaris submarine.

criticism

Management is an illegitimate profession.

cubicle

1. A cubicle with a door could also be a workstation in an en-suite

2. A cubicle with a door could be an office

3. A workstation designed to turn eggheads into blockheads.

curiosity

1. Child-like quality of wonder destroyed by bureaucracies

2. Active ignorance, because you don't know what you're getting yourself into

3. ?

customer

1. A consumer with ambition

2. A client with humility

3. An annoying individual or group whose sole

aim is to interfere with perfectly good processes, systems, products and services.

cut-rate

Surgery for inflamed prices.

CV

1. The most creative work of fiction that a manager is ever likely to write, revealing himself to be a team player, a bushwalker, Rotarian, dubiously educated, and a good family man every Wednesday night and on alternate weekends

2. Check Value

3. Control Value

4. Computer Virus

5. Cardio-Vascular

6. Control Volume

7. Cost Variance

8. Controlled Vocabulary

9. Command Vehicle

10. Cache Verification

11. Authored by a cut-rate cynic.

cynic

Someone who sees not only that the emperor has no clothes, but also that there is, in fact, no emperor.

Dad jokes

I tell Dad jokes. He likes them.

data

Information that is useless until contextualised by more data, as two data points make a trend. More than two is overkill.

data-mining

1. Drilling down
2. Using the vertical to make sense of the horizontal.

(*See* **core values**)

data-processing

Warehousing irrelevant information.

deadline

1. Something you miss, like nostalgia
2. Something to die for.

deal

1. Something to do with the cards you've been dealt

2. Something to cut

3. Something you can agree to today, and renege on tomorrow

4. An ideal ordeal.

death wish

Desire to be CEO.

debit

Money to be repaid if and when possible.

debriefing

1. Like detoxing, deconstructing and dismantling, debriefing assists stressed employees to forget their original brief

2. Making things longer.

debt

(*See* **bad debt**)

decentralisation

The road to anarchy.

(*See* **centralisation** *and weep*)

deception

Authentic lying.

decision

1. What happens when you are stuck with alternatives

2. What happens when there are no alternatives

3. What happens when there is no alternative

4. A choice made some time in the future or in the past, by someone else, based on false assumptions and incomplete data.

decision-making

Choosing management activities on the basis of power rather than expertise.

decision theory

The theory that theory can help decision-making in practice. Experts are undecided.

defamation

Honesty.

defenestration

The false axiom, held as true by Apple users, that without Microsoft everything would be better.

deficit

An optimistic loss.

definition

Found in dictionaries and contradictionaries, where it serves this purpose.

deflation

Pricking the bubble of pretentions of inflated economists. It is the proper antidote to inflation, and all arguments against deflation are wrong.

delegation

Getting other people to do your leg work.

de-merger

1. Waking up

2. Re-acquisition.

democracy

1. A mate and me singling you out, making you the minority, and doing whatever we want to you, writ large and thought to be just

2. Some entities which pay tax but do not vote –e. *g.* foreign corporations, or individual non-voters – can influence politicians and their parties' policies

3. No government is better than democracy

4. The reality is that even those who are not party to a decision can vote; *e.g*, voters who do not pay tax have an equal say to those who do

5. The assertion that all parties to a decision have an equal vote, irrespective of ability, knowledge, relevance, intention, vested interest or belief in democracy

6. Votes do not have equal weight in a democracy. If you vote for a losing candidate, then your vote is worth nothing. If you vote for a winning candidate and the candidate wins by more than one vote, then your vote is worth nothing. If your vote is the decider in a one-vote victory, then you become a dictator.

democrat

The type of manager – the darling of the HR departments – who includes HR departments in all strategic decisions, verifying and validating the HR department and the concept of HR itself.

demographics

Endless dissections of the market requiring continuing finessing, advocated by researchers paid hourly, as a way of predicting which products will sell where, instead of just marketing to the general population and letting them sort it out for themselves.

demystification

The belief that all beliefs are better if explained, except the belief in demystification.

denial

Hair-trigger response to media enquiries.

departmentalisation

Reorganising failed groupings in the hope that shuffling the card deck will produce a better hand. Promoted by managers incapable of improving profits or efficiencies in order to put their stamp on an organisation and so move up the ladder.

depreciate

What happens to your money as a result of inflation, itself caused by governments printing money, so that whilst there is more of it about, each unit is worth less.

depression

An economic term for a recession that hits you personally. Also a psychological term for what happens to you after you're hit by the economic effect.

deregulation

Government allowing business to make its own mistakes.

deviant

Heretic who questions the religion of management.

devotee

(*See* **deviant** *above, and antonymise*)

dialogue

1. Listen to me and nod if you agree

2. A phone log

3. An explanation in a box.

dilemma

Deciding whether to use decision theory.

dilettante

A male manager who subscribes to the opera, and sometimes even goes with his own wife.

diploma

Certification of continuous improvement along a continuum of graduated degrees, which shows nothing but proof of payment.

diplomacy

1. The ability to smile while saying nothing at length, in several languages, to people you detest

2. A sea of diplomas.

direction

1. Something that you give, but never receive

2. Where we're heading, as determined by the straight line from where we've been, through where we are now and into the infinite future

3. An excuse for a conference ever since some Roman asked: *Quo vadis?*

disambiguate

1. To systematise conjointly and coequally

2. To categorise

3. To cloud

4. To clarify

5. To classify

6. To make unclear in a whole new, intellectually intimidating way.

disciple

1. Someone who believes that the originator of the latest management fad is a guru

2. A junior manager with ambition.

discipline

The power that a guru has over a disciple to suspend thinking and engage in whimsical rule-following.

disclosure

In contradistinction to full disclosure, this is the selective revealing of self-serving data.

discounted cash flow

The sum of money received over time, after it has been ravaged by ongoing devaluation.

discrimination

1. The subversive acknowledgement of differences
2. A quality that allows for the recognition of quality.

disequilibrium

A word best left in the dictionary.

disintermediation

A work relationship with no intermediaries, such as when manufacturers deal directly with customers. The nature of this concept is disconcerting to managers managing to manage managerial management practices, as it exposes their role for what it is: not an expeditor, facilitator or even catalyst, but rather a hindrance, obstruction and impediment to serving the organisation and customer.

distribution

An allocation that you receive in order to head off retribution.

distrust

Due diligence.

dividend

1. An amount of money just large enough to stop you from selling your shares

2. The end of the divide.

divine plan

A plan of which you're unaware.

division of labour

Workflow arrangement designed by top management to ensure that an inverse relationship exists between the value of work done and remuneration for it.

doctorate

What you do with someone else's data.

do-nothing decision

Say no more.

doubt

We hesitate to offer even a tentative definition.

downmarket

A position attractive to astute consumers unconvinced by branding.

downsizing

Being linguistically sensitive when rightsizing, outsourcing or offshoring.

dream

1. Memorable sleep

2. Thinking that managers matter. (Having a vision.)

drill down

To actually find out what's below the surface of a problem. As in mining, data-mining, biopsies and autopsies, some of the information will necessarily be destroyed in the process; this is the Observer Effect.

(*See* **data-mining**)

driver, personal

Your auto motive.

duck pâté

Quackamole.

due diligence

Approving of what you are buying.

(*See* **caveat emptor**)

duty

Archaic concept connoting an obligation to do the right thing, now performed only by garbage collectors.

e.g.

An example, for instance.

early riser

The early bird catches the worm, but the early worm gets eaten.

e-commerce

1. An internet-based form of value creation in which the usual economic and accounting measures do not apply, except if you need cash, in which case you are forced into a state of involuntary recreation

2. Eeking out a living in the virtual world.

econometrics

1. An invalid, non-theoretical and incorrect 'discipline': there are no constants of human behaviour, measures of quantity are historical and utility is not intersubjectively comparable

2. Making assumptions about assumptions, and assigning number to them.

economic

(adjective) Parsimonious.

economics

1. The study of the logical implications of human action

2. The multiple of economic

3. Known for very good reasons as the 'dismal science'.

economies of scale

The argument, put forward by economists, that buying, selling or making lots of the same thing makes the whole process profitable, when fewer numbers would be sub-economic.

economist

1. It depends
2. An economic mist
3. Something the economy missed
4. A 'dismal scientist'.

education

What people use to develop a talent for training, and the ability to see through and go beyond it.

effective

1. Strategic implementation
2. Implemented strategy
3. Strategic strategy
4. Implemented implementation.

(*See* **efficient**)

efficient

The expeditious and tactical implementation of the wrong strategy.

(*See* **effective**)

egalitarianism

The belief that all subordinates should submit equally. Being able to address your boss by his first name.

egoist

An eye for an I.

elitist

The very best team player: the player who plays with the team.

ellipsis

1. ...

2. Periodic detention

3. Text type lacking in dash.

4. There's no end to it

5. An illustration of the importance of the rhetorical device of grouping things in threes.

eloquence

Teflon quality of CEOs to smooth over mistakes with words.

email

1. Medium for the manufacture and distribution of trivia

2. Spam-generator

3. A dis-missive

4. Gender neutral sin tax.

emotional intelligence

The ability to know when to be emotional, when to be intelligent and when to cry.

empowerment

Letting people think that they're doing what they want by empowering them with the word 'empowerment', while they work for you under your direction.

end, the

enlightenment

1. Lying in the sun without getting sunburnt

2. The incorrect belief that thinking is good –

   - because there are more good ideas than bad ones, and

   - because good ideas are more persuasive.

entrepreneur

1. Someone who makes a virtue out of improvisation. Like an actor who can't learn lines, an entrepreneur doesn't work well with others but often gets the best roles and the biggest laughs.

2. In a 'lean startup', think of the 'repeatability model', and remember that you're 'playing to win'. Always looks for adjacencies to your core business, but beware of mission creep – oh, wait, looking for adjacencies is mission creep. Rapid prototyping, or failing fast and failing often, is very important. In other words, whatever you do, don't succeed. Being a successful entrepreneur requires persistence, I mean pivoting, not persistence. Whatever you do, avoid persistence. More important than knowing where you are playing, is knowing where you are not playing. In other words, the more potential business you reject, the better.

error

One who errs.

(*See* **mistakes** and **omissions**)

error-free

A claim made by software engineers to show that they have a sense of humour.

erudition

Wisdom's rude awakening.

estimate

A claim made by business planners to show that they have a sense of humour.

ethics

The last recourse of CEOs to explain what went wrong.

evaluation

Using the divining rod of the retrospectroscope to determine who did what well when.

evidence

What I learnt in the lift on the way here.

examination

1. Politically incorrect performance discrimination. Under attack because it is a vehicle for failing students and thus discriminates against those with low ability

2. The only test of knowledge gained, as distinct from plagiarised essays, syndicate groups and computer simulations. Produces so much anxiety that normally self-contained students find that the competition between their intellect and bladder requires frequent trips to the privacy of the bathroom cubicle to consult the notes taped to their chests.

excellence

Quality pursued by CEOs who believe that they should be addressed as Your Excellency.

excuses

Lists of woe. See below.

excuses for doing an MBA

1. You want to understand the latest management thinking

2. You want to meet like-minded aspirants, and develop a network of soul mates, fellow

travellers and high achievers who can help you reach your goals

3. Your career has stalled

4. You really want to do a DBA, but don't yet have the grades.

excuses for arriving late to work

1. You attended the early morning funeral of your last boss

2. You applied mouth-to-mouth to a co-worker suffering hyperventilation at the pub after work yesterday, and the wrong impression was given and had to be explained at length over breakfast

3. You ran into your boss's boss and spent a lot of time praising your boss, and didn't want to leave out any details

4. You were awake all night writing a work report and didn't realise that it was time to go into the office. And besides, it would be disrespectful to arrive before the boss.

excuses for having a messy desk

1. A clean desk means that your drawers and filing cabinets are full of junk

2. Looking at one piece of paper at a time is

inefficient, and indicative of an inability to multi-task

3. If your desk is clean, co-workers may think that you're about to change jobs. Anyway, I alone know where everything is. That's called job security

4. A messy desk in and of itself is a useful excuse for many other parts of your role: files, invoices, telephone message, meeting minutes and your diary can all be lost as required, and simultaneously be within easy reach should a real need arise.

excuses for not winning that sales pitch

1. You weren't prepared to spend the company's money on a loss leader, and the opposition undercut you on price

2. They didn't understand your ideas and they are so far ahead of their time

3. You thought that the submission deadline was just a rough indication

4. You chose the spaghetti bolognaise at the selection lunch, and it splattered all over the tender documentation.

excuses for failing at any work task

1. Colleagues let you down

2. The organisation didn't resource you

3. The photocopy firm, or the courier, or the consultant, or the computer genius didn't do what they promised they would

4. Whilst you are capable of carrying out most assignments, this was the one area in which you felt out of your depth.

excuses for being back late from lunch

1. You think that the deal is pretty well sealed now that you've wined and dined the prospective client

2. You were covertly listening to the opposition who were having their strategy retreat at the same coffee shop, and you felt that industrial espionage was a higher priority

3. You were stuck in an elevator, or in a traffic jam, or in a queue at the post office, or you were at the bank and it was held up and the police had to interview you

4. There was a fire alarm at your last appointment before lunch, and you were legally required to hang around for a head count

5. You had a late breakfast, not a late lunch, so get your facts right.

excuses for doing non-work related activities on your work computer

1. All work and no play…

2. Connecting with the outside world is motivating, and therefore your productivity actually increases, so this apparently irrelevant web-surfing or emailing or job application writing is, in fact, in your employer's interest

3. You need to find out what inappropriate activities other people are doing so that you can ask them to stop it

4. In an holistic cosmos, everything is interrelated, and you resent the implied distrust.

excuses for having a day off work

1. You took the boss's instruction to think more, literally, and spent a whole day being pensive

2. You were benchmarking how well your department had systematised workflow to cope with an unexpected service delivery supply reduction

3. You didn't. Denial can be an effective rebuttal. The person making you accountable may them

become defensive and owe you lots of brownie points

4. You were at the other worksite. This time-honoured method relies on having another worksite. Don't become confused and think you still in your old job. Remember, they sacked you for falsifying leave records.

excuses for getting married

1. You are in love, and don't know if it will ever happen again

2. You are loved, and don't know if it will ever happen again

3. You want to receive empathy from your subordinates, so that you can get them to work harder

4. You need to regulate your hitherto erratic social life, in order to be a productive corporate team member.

excuses for having children

1. My partner and I were bored with each other, and we felt that kids would keep the relationship alive, and there seemed little downside in testing the theory

2. We did a cost-benefit analysis, and they seemed better value than renovating the house

3. They would be company for the dog when we were at work

4. We needed the aggravation

5. It wasn't solely your fault

6. It was an investment decision: we hope that parenthood will pay off during our retirement.

excuses for arriving home late

1. The boss needed someone from the team to attend an executive meeting about the group's future viability, and I was selected as the most persuasive member

2. You met an attractive salesperson, had a few drinks, booked a room at a hotel, made passionate love and then had a romantic, candle-lit dinner, though not necessarily in that order

3. You had a consultation with a marriage guidance counsellor

4. You went to the kids' school, as you thought it was parent-teacher night.

excuses for getting divorced

1. Your married life was interfering with the business cycle, especially year-end reporting

2. You had some extra cash and didn't know what to do with it

3. You did the maths, and discovered that two really can't live as cheaply as one

4. You wanted to have an affair, and your spouse wouldn't let you.

excuses for changing jobs so often

1. You have tried to broaden your experience base to bring to each new role a broad understanding of how the industry as a whole works

2. Your former boss accused you of sexual harassment, and wasn't convinced by your feeble attempt to laugh it off: 'For me, harass is two words'

3. Your diligence showed up colleagues as lazy, and they white-anted you

4. You embrace change, and whilst terribly loyal, always look for opportunities to grow, both as a person and as a professional.

executive

1. Someone who executes executive decisions

2. A senior disempowered employee, one level below someone with authority

3. Someone who executes subordinates' careers.

executive summary

1. Writing for illiterates

2. The bit that is actually read.

existentialist

1. The essence of nothing

2. One who discovers that the egress is no exit.

exit interview

Showing an interviewee the door.

expenditure

The catalogue of excuses for where the income went.

experiment

Human resource management.

expert

1. Someone who stayed at university one degree longer than you

2. What non-experts call themselves and each other

3. Someone better paid than you are

4. A well-credentialed and expensive person from

somewhere prestigious, who says the obvious with much eloquence and at great length.

expertise

The qualified stripping away of certainty.

exploitation

The exploits of successful CEOs.

facilitator

An *agent provocateur*.

factory

A place full of humans but devoid of humanity.

facts

The theory that things exist.

fad

Your enemy's management philosophy.

fail

Something you can't let pass.

failure

The survivorship bias belief that what doesn't kill you makes you stronger. Often used positively, especially in the startup world, by salaried 'entrepreneurs' who have lost other people's money.

fairness

1. What happens to blondes
2. Blondes of any gender profiled as the fairer sex
3. Being blonde in any state.

faith

Rational belief in the irrational, and/or *vice versa*.

fallacy

The mistaken view of male superiority.

family

1. Prized distraction from the main game
2. Labour you don't get paid for.

fast-track

Road to unqualified disaster taken by queue-jumping MBAs.

favours

The real currency of management. That is, politics.

faux

A fair-weather fax.

fax

Tantamount to the verisimilitude of the approximation of the facsimile of the real thing.

feedback

A way of burying complaints in an alphabetical manner.

feminism

1. A style of corporate architecture characterised by structures with glass ceilings

2. The desire to get balls by castrating men

3. The recognition of females as isms, not ologies.

feminist

Feminists want doors to be opened for them.

finance

The name of the executive or department who or which can predict the past. Usually acts as a disapproving parent to the adults in operations and the children in marketing.

financial institutions

1. Insurance companies and their insurers, the reinsurance companies, and their insurers – oops, they're not insured, so someone has to bear the risk... oh that's right, the customers via exorbitant premiums

2. Non-banks masquerading as banks while evading regulatory authorities' regulations and authority.

fine print

1. Justification for lawyers' billable hours

2. Terms and conditions that are deliberately hard to read and understand

3. Footnotes of history

4. Endnotes of geography

5. Penalty for literacy.

first-line supervisor

A boss who you can actually see and talk to.

fiscal policy

How government earns unearned income and plans to misspend it.

fixed capital

Money someone senior to you has already allocated.

fixed costs

Expenditure items that you can't do anything about.

flattery

1. Praise for the vanity of managers
2. Verbal gas released at high pressure through a narrow opening
3. Phonetic philately fishing for the imprimatur of a stamp of approval.

focus

The ability to see what's going on when everyone around you is screaming 'Fire!' – unless of course there really is a fire, in which case the locus of your single focus hocus-pocus makes you toast.

focus group

A roomful of opinionated citizens whose views are meant to represent the millions of prejudices held by the whole world or some smaller market segment. Given that 37.46 percent of the data from quantitative research is made up on the spot, qualitative research is a more cost-effective way of coming up with authoritative, inaccurate information.

forecasting

A predictive activity popular since Biblical times, and even before, which is a testament to its popularity. The chances of success have remained constant for millennia.

foreign

1. Strangers at first sight

2. Putting the Zen into Xavier

3. Taking the Zen out of xenophobia

4. A wordsmith with his kith at the zenith of a monolith.

foreigner

1. Any driver slower than you

2. Someone who speaks management as a second language.

foreman

A boss with a better shirt than a first-line supervisor, but who still has no power.

formal organisation

One where 'casual Friday' was tried and convicted, but not executed.

fortune

1. What some make and others spend

2. When income exceeds expenditure.

franchising

The linking of small franchisees to make them operate like one large business, by giving franchisees all the risk and middle managers the authority of executives and the responsibility of the front-line workers, while the franchisor yields the highest returns.

fraud

1. The myth that managers are worth what they pay themselves

2. Freudian slip.

free market

Where goods are sold to people who want them at prices they are prepared to pay. You can see how different government is.

free-trade agreement

1. Truce between governments
2. Trade without government intervention.

friendly fire

In the military, this refers to the accidental killing of troops from one's own side. In business, this organisationally self-destructive behaviour is often provoked by managers whose sloppy and corrupt style goes unnoticed in a crisis. 'We made that decision in *the fog of war*' is the favourite excuse of the friendly fire manager.

full disclosure

Stupidity. Fool disclosure.

fundamentals

The rudiments and building blocks of a management practice, without which it would be rootless, insubstantial, vacuous, facile and gratuitous. No-one knows what these elusive elements are, but when articulated and elucidated, everything will be made clear.

game

1. Invented by managers for fun

2. Simulation stimulation situation

3. Re: veal

4. The theory that criminals only have dilemmas when they become prisoners.

gender

On forms, often confused with sex, which is not an option.

general manager

So called because he's not good at anything in particular.

(*See* **specialist**)

gibberish

1. The official language of public relations consultants

2. Capital communiqués

3. Like gibber

4. Malevolent retractable patois.

global

Aspirational assertion of intent to sell or work further afield, such as in the next office building.

glossary

Something to gloss over.

goals

The line of failed past objectives that form a trajectory of future points to aim for.

going forward

Not yet. Compare **moving forward**, which means never.

good employee, a

Not in popular currency.

government

1. A protection racket masquerading as a charity

2. A tax on both our houses.

greed

1. Good: agreed

2. Not giving in to the envious

3. Not giving to the envious

4. Not giving in to the jealous

5. Not giving to the jealous.

gross

1. Not nice

2. Earnings before profit is taken away.

groupthink

1. A disciplined lynch mob

2. The collective wisdom of empty skulls

3. A con census.

growth

Lump on the credit side of the balance sheet, usually appearing at the time of the CEO's remuneration review, before the bulge is moved to the debit side and the CEO is given a payout equivalent to the gross national product of a small Third World country.

guarantee

The fine art of standing by your product or service, subject to the fine print.

guesstimate

Easily evaded, eerily educated excusable estimate.

guru

1. A titled person who preaches what you believe you are entitled to

2. Roo goo versed in vice

3. A wise old man wise enough to grow old

4. A leader who gets others to snake-wrestle for the oil.

gut feeling

1. Tummy-ache

2. Foreplay between the overweight; (circles don't tessellate)

3. The basis for truly effective decision-making

4. Something you don't learn… in tuition.

happiness

An imaginary state much favoured by unhappy social scientists at dinner parties.

hard work

1. Substitute for ability

2. Antonym of management.

head-hunter

Executor, matchmaker, cannibal and sometimes pimp, who shaves the edges off square pegs so that they can be jammed into round holes long enough for the finder's fee to be paid.

hero

Someone who protects the company from its managers.

hierarchy

Cascading ranking created in the image of those at the top, to remind all others that they are not. This explains why leaders are in a constant state of anarchy, as there is no one above them. Hierarchies have more strata on the way up.

hierarchy of needs

The ranking of human requirements by psychologists, with psychological assistance required to reach high levels. This ensures high fees for the rapists *(sic)* therapists.

high-tech

1. Description of any inanimate object more complicated than a paper clip, and not as reliable

   2.   An automatic waiver.

history

1. Accidental banalities of the past, listed in chronological order

2. Stories that glorify their writers.

(*See* **minutes**)

holiday

Like **retirement**, proof of poor job selection.

home shopping

1. Buying things that you don't need from the comfort of your own credit card

2. Looking for somewhere to live, from where you live.

honesty

Socially acceptable lying.

hope

Believing that you will succeed in your next job.

horizontal integration

Buying organisations like yours so that you don't have to compete with them. However, even though you might own firms in your industry stratum, your whole business will be better off if each part of it competes with all others. So you may as well not integrate horizontally. Just lie down until the compulsion goes away.

hospitality

One bite away from hospital management.

hostile takeover

Takeover.

hot-desking

Renting corporate real estate by the human resource, thereby exchanging one cubicle for another.

housekeeping

Doing unto your own before they do unto you, so that you may jointly do unto others.

HR

People in the workplace, so-called because a Human Resource is easier to under-resource, ignore, downsize, rightsize or outsource.

human relations

My relatives, but not yours; your relatives, but not mine.

human resource

Person available for manipulation by the organisation.

human resource (HR) manager

Someone whose job it is to divide the workforce into misanthropes, misandrists and misogynists.

humanitarian

Manager who knows the PA's name.

hygiene

1. A factor in the productivity of workers, which says that unless you pay folk well, they won't be motivated to do well, but that paying people really well doesn't marginally increase output. Not fashionable among remuneration committees voting themselves large bonuses, nor among behavioural scientists who've looked at the original research methodology

2. What organisations have when the clean out their HR departments

3. Washing your hands after sacking someone

4. Washing your hands after outsourcing someone's role

5. Washing your hands after offshoring someone's role

6. Washing your hands after downsizing someone's role

7. Washing your hands after rightsizing someone's role

8. Washing your hands after outsourcing someone's role

9. Washing your hands after shaking a subordinate's hand

10. Washing your hands after shaking a superior's hand

11. Washing your hands after shaking a peer's hand

12. Washing your hands after shaking a customer's hand

13. Washing your hands after shaking a client's hand

14. Washing one of your hands after touching the other one.

hypocrite

Manager who claims he's a leader.

hypothesis

The finding of management consultants.

hysteria *(derived from the Greek word for uterus)*

1. A form of melodrama invented by men to cope with the female sense of humour

2. A form of melodrama invented by women to cope with the male sense of humour.

I

The supreme object of love.

ID

1. Giving people numbers instead of names. This is actually a more personalised form of identification, as numbers are more numerous than names

2. Good for the ego

3. Necessary for the superego.

ideal

My deal.

ideas

1. What managers outsource

2. The belief that managers think that they think

3. Only ever thought of when you don't have any.

identity

When you become your business card.

ideology

1. Ideas – but not ideals – used to promote management as a profession

2. What managers follow

3. What leaders suspect.

idiot

1. An utterly foolish individual who has, therefore, risen to the top of his profession

2. A member of powerful sect whose influence in politics has always been dominant

3. What a manager thinks the consumer is

4. What a consumer thinks a manager is

5. What one manager thinks another manager is

6. What a leader thinks a manager is

7. What a pedant thinks a writer who ends a sentence with 'is' is.

i.e. *(inarticulateness explained)*

Admission that you have failed to communicate clearly the first time, and that you are looking to blame and patronise the reader by re-stating your original point in simpler language. In other words, 'in other words'.

ignorance

The state of knowing that you know nothing, which is more than others know.

(*See* **idiot**)

illiteracy

1. Entry criterion for admission to an MBA program

2. Entry criterion for admission to an MBA programme.

illusion

Seeing your team nodding in agreement when they're nodding off.

imagination

The ability to think with your mind's eye about something not actually present. Not recommended to be used whilst operating heavy machinery or driving. Or anywhere in the corporate world.

immorality

Postmodern amorality.

implementation

Something best left to middle management, as its accountability quotient is dangerously high for the CEO, the COO, the CFO, the CIO, the CDO, the CTO, the CMO and so on.

imports

Traditionally come from overseas.

impossible

Managerial self-development.

imposter

A manager who can't spell.

impostor

A manager who aspires to executive status.

incentive

One hundredth of a dollar.

incentive system

Yelling: 'Work harder, you bastards!' When this is deemed politically incorrect, more emotionally damaging structures are put in place, such as the practice of the **most** efficient managers being routinely de-hired.

incompetence

People-orientated, collegial, compassionate, democratic, emotionally intelligent, management-schooled, liberal-minded, flexible, open-minded, visionary modus operandi.

incompetent

Antonym of Machiavellian.

indecisiveness

1. Um…

2. Teamwork, delegating, democracy, research, empowerment…

indemnity

Insuring yourself against your own incompetence.

independence

Quality of the loose cannon who fires broadsides at meetings.

independent

Something that still entails source, selection, sponsor and style.

indifference

1. Turning a deaf ear to customers' complaints. A suggestion box without the box

2. Being cool.

individualism

Belief in the value of the individual, especially when no-one agrees with you. Inconsistent with the practice of management.

industrial espionage

Competitive research.

industrial psychology

The use of a caring profession in an uncaring way.

industrial sociology

The use of a non-caring profession in a caring way.

industry

A sector that works.

industry relations

The forced tripartite relationship between government, employees and employers, based on the misconception that they have common goals. Best to let consumers work it out.

inertia

The closest thing to stability achieved by most organisations.

inflation

1. An increase in the quantity of money

2. Another form of taxation without consent

3. The creation, by government, of less from more.

information

News to abuse.

information technology

Software-hardware integration, into which randomly selected knowledge is placed temporarily, only to see it irrevocably transmuted into meaningless gibberish upon output.

infrastructure

The synthesised vertices and integrated, interconnected interfaces of the meta-architecture of a system's physical resources, sometimes designed to dovetail with the nexuses of human resources, sometimes designed to supersede them.

initiative

Putting your initials to an action.

innocent

Not yet guilty.

innovation

Creativity you get paid for.

insanity

Inflexible idea that any individual manager is important, indispensable and irreplaceable.

insolvent

The state of being in sudsy liquid, where froth bubbles and vice versa, for the purpose of cleaning hard-to-remove stains from your balance sheet.

inspiration

Temporary insanity.

institution

Institute for incantation and decanting.

instructions

Managers telling managers how to manage.

insubordination

1. Clearing your throat during your boss's slide presentation
2. Clarifying to your boss what you thought they said
3. Free speech.

intangible asset

Something that you're happy to quantify when selling and to qualify when buying.

integration

Compelling competing business entities to work together.

integrity

Principled rectitude.

intellectual

The official enemy of managers. The first person to be shot, come the managerial revolution.

intellectual property

Where intellectuals live.

intelligence tests

1. Gauge of compliance – provides evidence of the intelligent refusal to do them

2. Superseded by emotional intelligence tests

3. Measure of proficiency at intelligence tests

4. Politically correct way of dividing them from us

5. Bag of tricks invented by psychologists; used by managers to assess entry into their profession, but excludes nobody.

(*See* **idiot**)

intentions

Potholes on the road to management.

interest

1. The price of time

2. Additional unearned money that you receive if you lend money, or the additional money that you pay on money that you borrow. The difference between these two interest rates should always be in the favour of the banks, as this is how they are funded. The cost of capital is equivalent to calculating it.

interim results

Retractable conclusions about financial performance.

internet

Communication medium for networking the depersonalisation of human contact.

internet access

What it takes you to realise that the information you are looking for is in your filing cabinet.

internet security

A continuous game between anti-virus and anti-spamming software developers, and 3 to 6 year olds auditioning for careers.

interview

A face-to-face meeting with a job candidate, before appointing the one most like the interviewer, her client or her boss.

intrapreneur

A manager pretending to be an entrepreneur, without risking his own capital.

in-tray

1. Open-cut recycling bin
2. Bottomless pit of tasks which would have been completed if your colleagues had been competent.

intuition

A catch-all defence when logic fails.

invention

Something created from the inventory.

inventory

Over-ordered stock.

investment

A gamble that hasn't yet paid off.

investment banking

The opposite of consumption banking, whereby the financial institution tries to make money from its customers.

invisible hand

Spontaneous order, in that organisations will prosper without management.

invoice

A document, valuable to the writer but inconsequential to the recipient, which makes an ambit claim on the latter's funds.

irreversible decision

One that will be enforced until it is overturned.

isms

A lower case study about the International Strategic Management Society.

issues management

Outsourcing an apology.

it depends

Disclaimer.

italics

jargon

Language used by managers to obfuscate, bamboozle and befuddle everyone, even themselves.

jargon generator

How it works –

Select three words, one from each column. This will create a three-word description of a project or a management theory. Repeat for each table.

For example, in the MBA jargon generator, you could construct an 'alphanumeric distribution market'. Sounds reasonable; means nothing: that's the joke.

You'll have 3,000 options to choose from. Colleagues, superiors and subordinates will admire your originality, hold your linguistic dexterity in their highest esteem, and look up to your adroit leadership style.

To be a jargon master simply master the jargon. Then, like these matrices, you'll be a jargon generator.

MBA		
alphanumeric	balance	data
annual	design	development
creative	distribution	forecast
ethical	finance	initiative
historic	marketing	market
integrated	morale	network
parallel	non-profit	output
resource	operations	process
scheduled	planning	review
workplace	sales	solution

consulting		
commercial	alignment	advice
competitive	based	change
conceptual	climate	clarification
cyclic	culture	focus
global	infrastructure	knowledge
intelligent	leadership	matrix
positioning	reinvention	model
strategic	re-purposing	paradigm
tactical	synergy	shift
worldwide	throughput	template

leadership		
collaborative	business	allocation
consultative	controlling	committee
cooperative	governance	implementation
empowered	government	meeting
management	international	metaphor

motivated	mission	outcome
organisational	productivity	project
shareholder	profitability	result
stakeholder	values	statement
team	vision	system

strategy		
dual	categorising	analysis
full	corporate	benchmark
input	e-commerce	calculation
macro	holistic	classification
micro	internet	idea
qualitative	mathematical	interface
quantitative	mentoring	nexus
quasi	partnering	re-engineering
semi	policy	report
total	synthesising	research

jealousy

I resent that.

job description

A list of some of the things that might be expected from you in your role, but not as important as the unexplained (and inexplicable) catalogue of tasks that you actually perform, especially being a scapegoat for your immediate boss's mistakes.

job dissatisfaction, or excuses for changing jobs

1. Your diligence showed up colleagues as lazy, and they white-anted you so often

2. You have tried to broaden your experience base to bring to each new role a broad understanding of how the industry as a whole works

3. You embrace change, and whilst terribly loyal, always look for opportunities to grow, both as a person and as a professional.

job enlargement

Giving you wider responsibilities without extra pay.

job enrichment

Giving you deeper responsibilities without extra pay.

job rotation

Swapping your crummy job for someone else's, without extra pay.

job satisfaction

1. A feeling promoted by executive search consultants when mere salary isn't enough

2. The pleasure given to people who enlarge, enrich or rotate other people's jobs

3. Something you spend

4. Indication of lack of initiative.

joint venture

Shared risk without shared returns.

junk mail

Slow spam.

just price

Price.

justice

Fair enough.

just-in-time manufacturing or production

Justification for a seat-of-the-pants management style unsupported by adequate stock reserves.

key player

An employee you can't sack before finding a replacement.

knee-jerk reaction

The tendency to knee a jerk in the reaction.

knowledge

What information is to data, knowledge is to information. This knowing ledge is an essential platform from which to escape a profit plateau.

knowledge worker

Human catalyst who traces the progress of data to information to knowledge to wisdom, and remains unaffected by the journey.

Labour Day

Twenty-four hours during which no work takes place, in order to celebrate the eight hour day.

laconic

Manner of speaking that makes inarticulateness a virtue.

laissez-faire

1. Planning to have no plan
2. Planning to have a plan
3. Lazy fare
4. The economic belief that business can do better without government help.

landlord

The lessor of two evils.

language

What distinguishes humans from animals, and what humans use to deny the distinction.

lateral mobility

Moving the unsackable sideways.

lateral thinker

A prostitute at performance appraisal time. A non-literal thinker.

lateral thinking

1. Horizontal thinking performed by a management philosopher

2. A lay down misere topic for a consulting project, training offsite, coaching topic or mentoring session

3. Being promoted sideways, and, at the end of the day, thinking that that can't be.

laughter

Honest response to a management decision. Perhaps this explains why there are so many yes-men (not to be confused with yes-women). Because you can say yes when smiling, but you cannot say no.

launch

The ritual celebration of the birth of a new product or service, at which the baby is sold to pay for contraception.

law

The logically defensible rules of conduct, which obviously cannot be a creation of government, and against which managers immunise themselves. Used to put entrepreneurs in jail and to frighten managers. Not applicable to leaders.

lawyers

1. Those who prosecute both sides of de fence

2. Justification for the existence of alternate dispute resolution

3. One of three groups of professionals, wedged between prostitutes and doctors, whom lawyers visit in sequence.

lay-offs

Weasel word for transferring the impact of management mistakes to subordinates.

laziness

Poor motivation.

lead by example

I am an example of good leadership; you should lead like I lead. Then there'll be no followers…

lead time

The time between completing one prerequisite task and commencing its successor, minus the time taken to calculate it.

leader

If a manager is someone with paid followers, then a leader is someone with unpaid followers who will jump over the cliff with them, or even for them.

leadership

1. The relationship between the led and those who want to bewitch them

2. What a leader does. And a leader shows

leadership. Only a leader can see this apparent paradox as truth. The corollaries of this statement are:

- if you think this reasoning is circular, you'll never make it to top management, and

- if you're not confused, then you really don't understand what's going on.

learning curve

1. A rounded education

2. A metaphor of a graphical representation of exponential acquisition

3. Turning educational corners

4. An educated guess.

learning opportunity

1. A failure. There is no absolute failure, except the failure to say that your failure is not a learning opportunity

2. Anything and everything.

learning organisation

Potential customer for a teaching organisation.

lecture

A one-sided exchange of ideas between two parties, without passing through the minds of either.

legislation

A refuge for the white-collar criminal to retreat behind when explaining non-compliant corporate governance behaviour.

leisure

1. Making laziness a virtue
2. Mythical, idyllic time between jobs.

lending

The process of renting money to people who can't afford to buy it yet.

lesser evil

Bachelor of Business Administration.

level playing field

1. A surveyor's fantasy: a theodolite on a tripod
2. Where the goal posts were moved to.

liability

1. A pain in the asset base
2. The amount that you paid for an asset when you thought that it was worth more
3. A lapsed asset
4. A re-valued asset.

liberal-minded

Someone who believes that everything is relative, including the claim that 'everything is relative'.

(*See* **idiot**)

library

Place where homeless people watch TV.

lifelong learning

Slow learners.

lifetime warranty

(*circular reasoning*) A worthless guarantee which states that as long as the product is working, you'll fix it, and that as soon as it is broken, its lifetime is over, and, consequently, so too is its warranty.

limited liability company

A business entity whose shareholders are limited and a liability to society.

liquidate

To make a liquid from a solid by letting off steam.

listening

Time to think of what you are going to say next.

literacy

1. People who understand the literal meaning of symbols. Uncharacteristic of postmodernism

2. Numeracy for the innumerate.

literature

A body of knowledge that professionals consult after they retire.

litigation

More paperwork. A liturgy to litter, literally.

logic

The art of reasoning imposed on psychiatrists by their patients.

logistics

1. The sequencing and measurement of queues, delays and excuses

2. A new word for very big trucks, created by the very big people who drive them, so no one's going to argue. The same goes for supply chain management, which refers to both truck drivers and their bosses, and to other big people in the shipping and airfreight industries.

long-range planning

Planning that includes planning as part of its planning.

long-term

The next reporting period.

loophole

1. A chance to keep your money whole

2. Incentive to read and be alooph

3. A polite arsehole

loss leader

The fallback justification to which you retreat when selling something below cost.

loyalty

1. The last domain of employees uncompetitive in the marketplace

2. Lack of ambition.

loyalty program

A plan to encourage customers to keep buying something when its intrinsic merit is not enough.

luck

Having a job with authority but no accountability.

(*See* **management consultant**)

Machiavellian

The art of managing people by lying to them and getting away with it, by (mis)quoting Machiavelli.

macroeconomics

Economists defending their income.

magic

Psychological tests.

management

1. What managers do until they become leaders
2. Manipulative surveillance.

management academic

Someone who conspires with management students in the shared misbeliefs:

- that management can be taught, and
- that management can be learnt.

Those who can: *do*

Those who can't: *educate*

Those who can't educate: *consult*

Those who can't consult: *profess*

Those who can't profess: *train*

Those who can't train: *research*

Those who can't research: *manage*

Those who can't manage: *lead.*

management by objectives (MBO)

Management by thinking about tomorrow instead of the day after.

management consultant

A highly educated unemployed person continually attending paid job interviews.

management retreat

1. Sexual harassment without the sex

2. A temple in which the religion of management is taught backwards.

management school

Enrolled in by executives whose high opinion of their own leadership potential is not shared by their superiors. However, if your career is failing, an MBA won't help.

management science

An oxymoronic description of management which assumes that all employees have read the same textbook: the one that the boss gave them.

managerialism

The self-defeating management program – misleadingly called philosophy – which demands that more than half the members of all work organisations be managers. The job of non-managers is to help managers achieve their KPI's, thus guaranteeing the latter's obscenely inflated salaries. The triumph of camp followers over warriors, and power over achievement. Replaces underpaid authoritative experts with overpaid authoritarian managers.

managing director (MD)

The least informed person in the organisation. Just managing.

manipulation

Comes between managing director and manual worker.

manual worker

Someone who can see the effect of his labour, usually derided by insecure workers who can't.

margin

The straight and narrow. See far left and far right, on this and other pages.

marginal cost

The cost of giving all workers a new ruler.

marginal utility

A ute in a ditch.

market economy

The market is the economy.

market research

An activity based on the false assumption that people will tell you what they will buy before they do, or that they even know what that would be.

market value

The fallacious belief that an agreed price can be determined before sale. It is the simultaneous denial and admission that the market value is what it is and cannot be known until then. Only through demonstrated preference can preference be demonstrated.

marketing

Matching impossible market wants and needs with unlikely organisational capability and capacity.

martyr

Someone who dies for an undying truth.

Marxism

The belief that all individuals, other than Karl Marx, are unimportant.

mass education

Training for taxi drivers.

materialism

When idealism doesn't matter.

matrix

A way of making words look like numbers; particularly useful if you are trying to hide data.

maturity

When a market or product cycle is more grown up than any producer or consumer in it.

maximum

1. The largest number possible using available resources, irrespective of profitability

2. A large maternal figure.

(*See* **optimum**)

MBA

1. Mistaken Business Acumen

2. Management By Acronym

3. Married But Available – the divorce course

4. Mind-Blowing Asset

5. Making Busy Arrangements

6. Main Battle Area

7. The misstep between BBA and DBA.

MBFA

Like Management By Wandering About – but more widespread.

me

Public I.

measurement

1. The transformation of managerial behaviour into take-home pay

2. A smartphone that is always-on is a measure of how poorly an employer thinks of an employee. A smartphone being on 'vibrate' is a measure of the employee's humiliation.

medals

Unqualified qualifications awarded as receipts for membership dues.

meeting

A form of occupational group therapy, whose purpose is to console people who cannot solve a particular problem alone by proving that no one else can either.

melodrama

1. The daily play of characters in the business pages, with managing director heroes being pursued by regulator villains, with industry associations cheering and trade unions booing from the sidelines

2. Vice versa.

memory

What managers lose when giving evidence before (but not after) government commissions.

mental disorder

Condition of someone found in the management section of bookshops.

mentor

Someone who meant well.

mentoring

Gossiping nostalgically. Giving back what you worked for.

merger

1. Euphemism for acquisition

2. When wedlock becomes deadlock

3. When deadlock becomes wedlock

4. The period prior to de-merger.

(*See* **synergy**)

metacognition

Thinking about thinking, which is procrastination. Improving yourself by separating yourself from your thoughts; when you separate the thoughts of others from their persons, that could be treating them as sex objects.

metaphor

1. A figure of speech in a manner of speaking

2. Like a simile

3. I'm sorry, my mind's gone blank.

metaphysics

Sub-editors who go above and beyond.

method

A system without a cycle.

microeconomics

Economic fine print.

midlife crisis

Panic-stricken realisation that you have not become what you wanted to be, and that you don't won't to be that person anymore.

millionaire

1. Manager with a large mortgage and three divorces

2. House-owner with neither a mortgage nor a divorce.

mind

Mythical entity with free will that replaces the soul as the spiritual centre of the individual. A bucket for thoughts, feelings, emotions, values, beliefs and memories. Source of peculiar, unconscionable, undiagnosable illnesses, diagnosed by corporate psychiatrists and industrial psychologists.

minutes

A work of fiction. The history of a meeting from the viewpoint of the minute-taker; the secretary of a meeting is therefore the most powerful person there.

misbehavioural science

The science of labelling employees who are misbehaving as having 'inappropriate behaviour', when they're really just being naughty; a pseudoscience whose practitioners believe that the facts of misbehaviour are wrong.

miscellaneous

Assorted sundry heterogeneous items that would be misplaced elsewhere.

mission statement

The aims of an organisation and what sort of service it intends to provide: both pugnacious and spiritual. Something you can tell your kids, and that only they will believe.

mistakes

Made by managers due to information provided by subordinates; made by workers due to irrationality.

mob

1. The collective noun for many kangaroos

2. The collective noun for many Australian lawyers

3. The collective noun for many kangaroo courts.

model

A theoretical construct which is meant to represent a slice of reality. There is no model of reality as a whole. All the pieces add up to contradictory realities. The whole is not greater than the sum of its parts, it is just that the elements are not contextualised and the whole created from them doesn't look like any component part. The main beneficiaries of models are the model makers, who, unless they are in the theatrical special effects business, may be management consultants, economists, strategists, policy analysts, planners or pretenders.

modus operandi

Roman management style.

mole

Employee having a friendly chat about colleagues with the organisational psychologist.

monetary policy

Determining that a dollar is worth 100 cents.

(*See* **fiscal policy**, *which disputes the math, and the maths, and the arithmetic that makes one the other*)

money

1. Something to pay taxes with
2. The buck stops here.

monopoly

1. Something that isn't a monopoly
2. Government's method for coping with competition.

moral courage

Like regular courage, but preceded by a fable.

morale

A happy way of corporatising depression and making it the responsibility of big pharma.

morality

My right to impose my definition of right on you.

moron

A person who lives (and sometimes dies) for 100 'likes' from other morons.

moronity

The moronic age we live in – dominated by reality TV, celebrity, the fame of nonentities, the cult of feeling, the denigration of the intellect, the disregard for logic, the vilification of evidence, smartphones and other vibrators, relativism, newsy post-truth truthiness, victimhood, the New Right, the New Left, the New Centre, and self-righteous ranters.

motivate

To make the lazy work hard. Never agree to have this impossible task included in your job description.

motivational speaker

1. Professional with a winning personality, and a fee structure to match. Teaches a form of psychology that he does not practice, and if he did, he would be even more boring than he is.

2. Someone who looks like a comedian, but does not tell jokes.

motivational psychology

The study of moving forward.

moving forward

Used by managers to keep one word ahead of their colleagues, who are merely moving.

multiculturalism

The belief that all cultures are of equal value and therefore of none.

multinational

1. An entity with no legal or ethical responsibilities in any one country

2. The private sector equivalent of the United Nations, but with a better bureaucracy.

multiskilled

The ability to simultaneously do your job while telling people that you're doing it.

multisourcing

The recognition that many other organisations are now better than your organisation at what you used to do.

multitasking

1. The disorder that promotes attention deficit hyperactivity

2. Insourcing.

mythology

The foundation of the management profession, undermined by comparison with real professions, such as banking, gambling and witchcraft.

nanotechnology

There was a nanotechnology lab that was doing so well, it had to move into smaller premises.

narcissism

A personality disorder possessed by those CEOs who try to persuade their managers to admire them even more than the CEOs admire themselves.

need

Means necessity when physiological; means nothing when psychological.

negativity

Something positive people are negative about.

negotiation

The shifting mix of cooperation and competition that precedes victory by the least ethical.

nepotism

Making family values pay off.

nervousness

The unpleasant feeling rightly experienced by CEOs at AGMs.

net

Earnings after profit is taken away.

networks

An interconnected, integrated synthesis of an holistic totality.

neurotic

Accepts that 2 + 2 = 4 but can't stand it.

neutrality

A position you can choose to share or not to share.

'never give up'

Perceived as tenacity by managers, intransigence by workers, stubbornness by spouses and stupidity by psychiatrists.

news

1. Vehicle for the expression of personal feelings

2. Medium for the listing of possibilities. For instance: 'Managers with MBAs may be more effective', the opposite of which is also true

3. There is no news.

newspaper

1. Something to hit the dog with

2. Useful at the base of a birdcage

3. Wards off melanoma at the cricket, when folded into a hat

4. Justification for lopping unsightly trees

5. Old-fashioned way to train bloggers

6. Helpful in the separation of fish from chips.

niche

A rut that you have come to terms with.

nightmare

A smiling politician shaking your hand.

non-executive director

An executive who doesn't work for the company he's working for.

non-profit organisation

A profitable business entity that would be unprofitable if subjected to taxes payable by a for-profit organisation.

nonsense

I disagree with you but I don't know why.

non-viable option

Reducing managers' salaries.

novels

Books with almost as much pride and prejudice as management reporting.

now

Soon-ish.

numbers

Used by the illiterate to baffle the innumerate.

obedience

Revealing lack of initiative by unquestioningly following orders.

objectives

Something against which to measure your unattained aims.

obligation

Getting into trouble for something that you didn't do. Or did.

obscenity

Dismissing someone on the grounds of personality, irrespective of performance on or off the field.

obsolete

Manager who doesn't use consultants, coaches or mentors.

old boys' network

Proof that life after high school is an anticlimax.

old girls' network

Proof that life after school is climacteric.

online

An economic reality with virtual income and actual expenditure, resulting in real losses.

open-minded

Empty-headed manager.

operations

The part of the business that actually produces things. If it wasn't for operations (also known as production) the finance and marketing and leadership teams would have nothing – and be nothing. Yet finance continues to be patronising by requiring operations to submit plans and targets and other irrelevant signs of submission, and marketing says that if the market doesn't know about the firm's output, all will be lost. In fact businesses existed for a long time with the financial trivia being done in leaders' spare time and marketing being carried out by actually serving customers.

opinion

1. Temporary malleable belief, available to be sur-rendered for one held by a superior

2. Something a manager gives, but never takes.

opportunities

(*See* **challenges**)

opportunity cost

Opportunity lost.

optimal solution

The one where you tell most of the truth and still get to keep your job.

optimism

1. Expecting everything to come out as expected

2. Excuse for laziness.

(*See* **pessimism**)

optimum

1. The number of products or services required to create the largest profit possible using the smallest quantity of available resources

2. Opting to keep mum.

(*See* **maximum**)

orator

Speaker who speaks expertly.

order

1. While there is chaos theory, there is no order theory, so let's forget it

2. It's got form.

organisation

1. A collection of disorganised individuals temporarily occupying permanent roles with transferable titles

2. An amoral entity responsible to unaccountable stakeholders.

organisation chart

A graphic representation of who is meant to report to whom. Straight lines show formal reporting connections between people who have no chance whatsoever of influencing each other. Dotted lines show multiple or indirect relationships between people who know that have no power over each other and therefore work together with reciprocal respect. Not all dotted lines are on the chart. For instance, the CEO's personal assistant has more power than senior executives.

organisational behaviour

They don't behave.

(*See* **success**)

organisational climate

Seasonally adjusted work environment that changes from minute to minute and person to person.

organisational culture

People and culture are the essences of organisations, so you must destroy both to make an impact, create a legacy and advance your career.

organization

An American organisation. Just like a normal organisation, but with more buzzwords.

other

Neither this nor that.

output

An input on the way out.

outsource

To reduce fixed costs by increasing variable costs.

out-tray

Someone else's in-tray.

overwork

1. The fine line between working too hard – and not hard enough

2. The two-hour executive breakfast; three-hour executive lunch; the four-hour executive dinner.

oxymoron

Self-contradictory, paradoxical two-word phrase, such as entrepreneurial management, lead manager or managerial leadership.

PA (personal assistant)

1. Someone to give your work to

2. Someone to talk to

3. Someone who keeps your gate

4. Someone who makes your long list short

5. A masculine Ma.

pain

What you feel when your PA is not IN.

paperless office

1. Evidence of off-site storage
2. Office you haven't moved into yet.

paradox

When a lawyer says: 'All lawyers are liars'.

parameter

Something that is bound to border on constraint.

paranoid

A manager who claims that you don't respect him, when indeed you don't.

parent company

Archaic organisational entity which implies subsidiary/head office rivalry and internecine warfare based on the centralisation of power.

participative management

A common hallucination, two drinks short of a shared vision.

partnership

A coalition of equals that uses the democratic decision-making process of majority rule. If it is a partnership of two, then one partner is redundant.

part-time

A way for organisations to cut down on their wages costs whilst attracting goodwill from a hoodwinked public. A part-time job structure is given to people with things other than work in their lives. Let us assume that two part-time workers are notionally half-time. They would usually work 60 percent of a full-time role each, due to changeover debriefings, felt guilt, and dedication, giving the organisation a 20 percent productivity bonus. This scandal must be exposed.

pathfinders

Managers who can find the way to the executive washroom.

patience

What you need in order to hang out for the next anti-climax.

payback period

The length of time that it takes to be back where you started from, before you risked what you did. If you had been risk averse, you'd be there already by doing nothing.

payment by results

Fiction; never happens.

pedant

1. Internal auditor with a penchant for purple
2. A self-censor.

peer group

Mutual excuse for conformity.

pending

Purgatory

per capita

A numerator for any productivity measure that requires humanisation.

perfect knowledge

The only thing we're certain we don't have.

performance

1. Sometimes used to denote positive achievement, but generally ignored in favour of personality

2. Acting as if you're working.

performance appraisal

Personality appraisal.

personality

What poorly motivated people have to fall back on.

personnel appraisal

A politically correct from of verbal abuse.

pessimism

1. Expecting everything to come out as expected

2. Excuse for laziness.

(*See* **optimism**)

philanthropy

Advertising targeted at the poor.

philosophy

Traditionally the love of wisdom, superseded by the love of power.

plagiarism

1. Standing on the shoulders of giants without calling them names

2. Applauding the illiteracy of internet scribblers by stealing

3. A tribute without attribution

4. Finding intellectual property before it is lost.

planned obsolescence

1. The only successful evidence of planning

2. The state of redundancy in which something needs replacing as soon as it's paid for. Excellent for IT gurus and marketers.

planning

A game plan to avoid work by prognosticating; variations include: strategic planning, business planning, financial planning, scenario planning, contingency planning, as well as Plan B and planned obsolescence.

plant

Along with the other physical resources of an organisation – property and equipment – plant constitutes the genuine asset base available to be frittered away by strategists, financiers and marketers.

'please wait, your call is important to us'

Fuck off.

pleonasm

Half of the management profession. Truncated tautology – any management phrase beginning with 'strategic'.

plot

Under the boardroom table.

police

Management consultants with guns.

policy

The answer to why we do what we do around here when there's no reason for it.

politeness

Insincere form of address used by gatekeepers and other frustrated actors.

political correctness

Opinions one may express without receiving a slap to the head. An oxymoron in a democracy; a pleonasm in a dictatorship (or even using more words than the optimum to communicate meaning).

positive reinforcement

Something you are really good at.

postmodernism

Nihilistic anti-philosophy and undergraduate fetish that claims that nothing is important except itself, and equates a pair of boots with Shakespeare. The triumph of bullshit over science. The standard by which nothing is judged, including itself.

postmodernist

Someone who believes that it is true that there are no truths and that it is a fact that there are no facts.

potential

What you, yourself, had before you were actualised.

poverty

1.   The absence of wealth creation programs

2.   The presence of wealth creation programs.

power

The central concept in management, as the disinclination to talk about it suggests.

practice

1.   Something managers correctly profess to do but which still doesn't make management a profession

2.   What's left of management after the recognition that it is neither science nor art.

pragmatic

Doing what the boss wants.

pragmatism

American philosophy of self-indulgence based on the assumption that truth is what works; much favoured by managers to legitimate their feelings and contradictory ideas: 'Does it work for you?'

precision

An incisive précis that cuts to the quick.

predatory pricing

Being so competitive as to force the competition to resort to name-calling, having crippled their production, marketing and financing processes.

pre-preparing

1. To prepare on someone else's time

2. Foreplay without the post-play. Or the play.

presenteeism

The syndrome of having people take a day off without drawing on sick pay.

press conference

A meeting between various in-house and external media people, at which agreement is sought on which version of the truth to tell their audiences.

press release

Periodic escape of information.

presupposition

Something that you were supposed to have supposed already, supposedly.

price

The maximum the seller can sell it for and the minimum the buyer can buy it for.

price cutting

Sacrificing profit for turnover, sales and market share, in the hope that being busy will make those you report to think that you are effective.

price fixing

Sensible agreement not to confuse consumers with too much choice.

price sensitivity

The falling off of demand at the slightest whiff of news of a price increase. Best to conceal the real price by bundling products and services, making price comparisons impossible. This technique is widely used in the IT and health insurance industries, among others.

price war

Just like a real war, but just.

principals

In schools or professional partnerships, leaders with responsibility but no authority, continually struggling with impossibly competing priorities.

principles

1. What you stand on as you disappear into the quicksand of corporate life

2. Dispensable ethical standards.

priorities

Tasks with varying levels of importance and urgency that you will get around to as soon as you've finished your work.

private sector

That part of organised society that is neither non-profit nor government, but funds both.

proactive

1. Always thinking about, planning for and resourcing your team to be aware of the myriad possible events that could affect your business, thereby atrophying all spontaneity, innovation and creativity

2. Transmogrifying depression (worry about the past) into anxiety (worry about the future).

probability assessment

Valid about the same proportion of times as tossing a coin will result in its landing on its side.

problem

What managers are paid to solve but actually create.

problem finder

1. Psychiatrist

2. Management consultant

3. Perfectionist.

processes

Things to put in place.

procrastination

1. Management style in favour of crastinating

2. Default management style.

producer

The consumer's best friend.

product

Unlike a service, something tangible and worthwhile.

product differentiation

Making the bells and whistles more important than the train.

production

The act of creating a product. Production processes are best left to engineers and concealed from the rest of the so-called management team.

productivity

1. Obtaining the same output from reduced input

2. Obtaining more output from the same input

3. Doing more or the same with less

4. The quotient of output over input

5. None of the above, but something nebulous that can be increased to turn an organisation around.

profession

1. Any occupation that requires pre-career and ongoing training, is accredited or self-regulated, pays its members less frequently than every

week or, in the case of some professions such as poets, artists and actors, never

2. 'The Professions', on the other hand, relates to accountants, auditors, actuaries, lawyers, doctors, dentists and the like, as compensation for their being the butt of most good jokes

3. Not management.

professional

Anyone other than a professor who professes to belong to a profession. Not a manager. People with tickets on themselves who believe that the term 'professional' should have a capital P.

professional disagreement

A misunderstanding that each party to an agreement is paid for, even if all viewpoints are wrong.

professional relationship

A relationship based on money.

profit

When income is greater than expenditure, the executive salary bonus system needs overhauling.

profit centres

Those parts of an organisation worth keeping.

program

A document that assists you with the plot. Subtitles are better. If policy is the strategy, then a program is a tactic in the implementation of that strategy; if strategy is the 'why', a program is the 'what'.

progress

Moving experience, for which there is no temporal evidence, in which the future is thought to be better than the past.

propaganda

1. Having a good look at something
2. A press release.

prospectus

Prospect: us.

Protestant work ethic

We're working on it. Pray for us.

prototype

That test product or service, with at least one fatal flaw, bug, glitch or fault line, which is worth leaking to your competitors.

provision for bad debts

1. Quantified pessimism
2. Qualified optimism
3. Marketing's mistakes transferred to Finance's problems
4. Honest assessment of clients' honesty
5. Permission for Accounts Receivable to fail.

psychiatrists

Professional drug dealers and the new jailers. Modern witch-doctors. Inventors of imaginary illnesses.

psychoanalysis

Putting the anal into psychology.

psychological determinism

We're not to blame.

psychological tests

Putting the litmus paper of the psyche into the snake oil of tyrants; widely used by managers to control other managers. A self-destructive enterprise if ever there was one.

psychology

A study of ghosts in the machine; popular with managers who use it to manipulate others, but are its first victim.

psychotic

Unlike the neurotic who upsets himself, the psychotic upsets others, and is thus locked up in the executive suite.

public policy

The general foundation of government practice as generally publicised to the general public. The real basis for government practice is, of course, never released, and always denied, even in the face of Freedom of Information legislation. When confronted with the facts, bureaucrats can happily shift focus, change the face of the issue and recontextualise by saying that the full picture cannot be known due to national security matters. And they can parade a General to verify that assertion.

public relations

When your relations with your public go badly, hiring a PR firm won't help.

public sector

A bite out of the private sector.

public service

An oxymoron that describes the self-sustaining, amoral bureaucracy that supports the political party or coalition of the day - and its politicians.

public transport

Arriving late.

purchasing power

The blackmailing of suppliers into squeezing margins and taking all the risk, by demanding loyalty, then threatening to withdraw their orders.

purpose

If there is light at the end of the tunnel, it could be glaucoma.

'put steps in place'

Outcome avoidance strategy.

quack

Pseudo-expert whose ducks are not all in a row and who is not even a duck.

quadrant

Consultants feel comfortable with four of anything, which is two more than managers feel comfortable with.

qualification

The experience of the inexperienced; the skill of the unskilled; the education of the uneducable.

qualitative

Incomprehensible word-heavy analysis.

(*See* **quantitative**)

quality

A standard that is temporarily satisfactory. Later on, you'll be ashamed of what you deemed quality. And so on it goes. Continual improvement leads to self-hate.

quality control

The quality quota allocation process, through which it is determined how much quality is necessary for a product or service to be deemed to have the quality of quality.

quality of life

If there's a heartbeat, you're working.

quantitative

Incomprehensible number-heavy analysis.

(*See* **qualitative**)

question

1. A place to use my answer
2. Often begins with 'who', 'why', 'where', 'when' 'what' or 'how', and ends in a metaphorical interrogative, which, if you're literate, or even numerate, will be perceived as a question mark: '?'

racism

The belief that all races are the same – even in their differences.

radical

A naughty management academic with tenure.

raise

An increase in an employee's wage or salary, based on their negotiation ability.

raison d'être

The reason for our debt.

rational

You agree with us.

rationalisation

Turning your whine into sour grape juice.

reactive

Normal management practice: to respond to real situations as they arise.

reality

Putting the 'i' into realty.

reasoning

Valuable technical skill, reasonably discarded when promoted to management.

reasoning, circular

(*See* **circular reasoning**)

reassessment

Doing a personality test for the second time after failing the first one.

rebrand

To brand again after branding failed the first time.

recognition

Rethinking someone's achievements out loud.

recycling

Reverse garbage and vice versa.

red tape

The bloody ties that bind: something bureaucrats unwind in and everyone else gets wound up in.

redundancy

What happens when your boss finds out what you actually do.

re-engineer

Engineer again to redesign you out of your job.

reference

Fictional praising of underperforming employees in order to remove them from your payroll without a redundancy package.

reform

1. Correct

2. Repetition without replication.

refund

Getting your money's worth.

reinforcement

Incentivisation of managers so that they behave like rats.

reinventing the wheel

Reinventing the wheel.

relationships

Temporary alliances between individuals, groups or organisations, which last as long as their interests are overlapping.

relativism

1. It all depends…
2. A form of nepotism.

relativity

The notion that all issues are merely part of larger ones.

relevance

The standard by which all education is judged irrelevant.

remuneration

Renumeration.

repeat business

Business.

repeat customer

Customer.

reporting mechanism

Managers burying feedback through the use of a mobile phone, gossip, a suggestion box or physical assault.

repositioning

Changing potential buyers' perceptions of a product or service by taking it upmarket or downmarket or varying its consumer context *vis-à-vis* its competitors, without altering it in any substantial way.

repression

Smiling at interviewers you would like to murder.

repurposing

Finding a new reason for an organisation to exist. Often a useful distraction if things are going badly. For a business, acquisitions are effective on this front. For a government, war will work a treat.

reputation

Suffers when one is promoted; destroyed when one becomes CEO.

research

Tantamount to the approximate verisimilitude of the facsimile of shared subjectivity masquerading as objectivity.

research and development (R&D)

A twin organisational function with its own inbuilt scapegoat subgroup. Research can blame development, and *vice versa*. A self-destructive loss centre used as window-dressing to quell criticism that the organisation is doing the same old things all the time.

reserves

A balance sheet item with a zero next to it. This shows that the organisation is aware and responsible. Where did the obscene amount go? To the managers themselves, for being so prudent.

resignation

Career limiting move, and perhaps employment suicide. Not recommended, as the victim forfeits redundancy and other payouts. Wait for them to sack you. Either way, your résumé is diminished.

resources

Consumable process inputs.

responsibility

(anachronism) Entailed by the freedom to choose to deny that we are free to choose.

rest

A cover for lack of passion, direction or incentive that serves as an excuse of last resort.

(*See* **holiday**)

restructure

A way to fire people you don't like. Favoured by management consultants because it is a project that requires no facts, logic or evidence to support it, and thus guarantees more employment for consultants.

results

Should be hidden until things improve.

résumé

Lying in acute chronological order.

retiree

1. Someone who chose the wrong job

2. Someone on their deathbed

3. A superannuated employee with enough superannuation

4. The subject of your jealousy

5. The object of your envy.

retrospectroscope

Device used by CEOs to predict the past.

return on investment (ROI)

How much you expect to receive in exchange for your investment. Usually you would hope for more than you put in, but as deals progress, many investors settle for a break-even result, making much commerce merely occupational therapy.

reverse engineering

1. Using the solution to retrofit the problem
2. An engineer going off the reserve.

rights

1. Ritual, self-serving incantation of 'What do we want… when do we want it?'
2. What lazy people go out of their way for.

risk

Everything.

rituals

Management conference where the important issues are resolved at the bar.

robotics

Replacing squeaky wheels with well-greased ones.

role model

1. When your biography is hagiography

2. Female executive with a low-cut dress

3. Male executive who wears shorts on casual Friday.

roles

The masks we hide behind to make us look like we know what we're doing.

rule of thumb

That people see things differently. If you make a fist and extend your thumb, some people will think that you are saying 'OK', and others are offended that you are asking them to 'sit on it and rotate'.

rules of the game

Machiavelli's *The Prince*.

sack

Something organisations give people who spend too much time in it.

safe

Receptacle used by managers in which to store such precious items as subordinates' psychological test results.

salary

Payment in exchange for work, to employees who believe that they are indispensable.

salary packaging

That happy state in which pre-tax and after-tax earnings coincide.

sales

1. An individual or group who or which creates the need to buy when, if that need had been inherently present, the sale would have gone through already

2. The process by which people are turned into customers, creating in them an awareness that they need something that they didn't even want before the sales process began.

scandal

1. PR failure

2. PR success.

schadenfreude

1. Taking pleasure in a competitor's troubles, even though their problems do not help you. One of many unattractive human attributes. So it's not your fault: enjoy!

2. Using this word in company, where you are the only one who knows what it means, and, with a whimsical smile, declining to explain it

3. A shard of Freudian glass, forming both a prism and a barb.

science

Body of knowledge based on logical reasoning discovered by dead white males; under constant attack by those who find it difficult and suspect it might be true.

secret fund

Entrepreneur's answer to government, spouse, ex-spouses and other creditors.

segment

Making a pizza of marketing.

self-centred

Being into yourself rather than beside yourself.

self-control

Emotional unintelligence.

self-esteem

Liking the person you love most.

self-help

1. Insourcing

2. People helping themselves to help themselves.

selfishness

Living alone.

self-leadership

Telling oneself to follow oneself and refusing to do it.

semi-autonomous work group

A collection of co-workers looking for direction.

seminar

1. A forum where the lecturer asks the questions

2. Turning a conference into a seminary.

senior management team

Oligarchy that thinks it is an aristocracy.

service

1. *(noun)* The value-add that differentiates products; missing from most sales processes

2. *(verb)* To repair or maintain a product that should not need repairing or maintaining.

sex discrimination

1. Taste

2. Being able to tell the sexes apart

3. Chastity or celibacy.

sexism

The belief that the sexes are the same – even in their differences.

sexual harassment

When a co-worker makes you think that harass is two words.

shared values

When there aren't enough values to go around.

shareholders

1. People with a legitimate interest in a firm

2. Suckers like us who believe that we can overcome share-trading transactions costs.

(*See* **stakeholders**)

short-term

As far as you can see.

simile

Like a metaphor.

simulation

A game just like the real thing, except that it isn't, and everyone playing knows it and plays accordingly.

skill

1. The missing link in management

2. Dyslexic assassin.

slavery

Industrial democracy.

small business

A business on the way up, or out.

(*See* **big business**)

social construction

The Pacific Ocean, until you are dropped in it.

society

What remains when individuals disappear.

sociocultural

The social and cultural layering of organised life, helpful in stratifying employees, suppliers and customers, so you know who – or whom - to send to the opera, who to send to the football, and who is going to be unimpressed by either or both.

spam

For more copies of this excellent book, please use the order form in the back.

span of control

The unbridgeable distance between top management and the people at the bottom who do the real work, measured in strata titles.

specialist

Opposite of manager; hence lowly paid.

speculation

An articulate punt, just shy of an educated guess.

spelling

Irrelevant pedantry.

Spillane

A management term unmasked to reveal its true meaning through humour. A compression of the words 'spill' and 'entertain'.

spin doctoring

1. Doctoring the truth
2. Sugaring bitter pills
3. Administering second best medicine while praying that no-one laughs.

spiritual intelligence

1. Praying for a higher intelligence
2. When spooks come visiting
3. Praying to a higher intelligence

4. Preying on the foolish

5. Overcoming the laws of physics by walking on fire

6. Going to hospital with third degree burns, to have the hyphen reinserted.

spy

Human resource manager.

stable workforce

Suggestive of a lack of other job opportunities.

staff

Disempowered junior employee, several strata below someone with authority.

stakeholder

1. A Dracula-like figure ready to drive a pole into the very lifeblood of the organisation, for its own good and for the good of the industry. *(Stake holder)*

2. A horticulturalist. *(i.e., ditto)*

3. In the broadest sense, anyone at all.

4. A dyslexic short-order chef. *(Steak holder)*

5. A plea to not 'stay hotter'. *(Stay colder)*

standards

Raising the bar and then leaning against it.

standing in the shoes of others

1. Footing the bill
2. Where one of you is redundant
3. Getting in the way
4. Being orthotic
5. Empathy with soul
6. Being rapport cousin
7. Being a foot soldier
8. Being a shoe thief
9. Being brought to heel by toeing the line
10. Justification for putting on socks.

statement

Announcing a sentence.

statistical significance

A result that is significant statistically but not in any other way.

statistics

Originally this meant data that support the State and its leaders, but this deceitful, selective application of quantitative information is now entrenched in organisational life with the same purpose. Three out of four people make up 75 percent of the population. 86.43 percent of all statistics are made up on the spot.

status

Suits.

step up

Something managers are inclined to do in an escalating manner.

stereotype

1. Used profitably by advertisers, unprofitably by social commentators

2. Double trouble

3. An understudy

4. An HR profile.

stoic

Whatever. In its modern form, a person with the philosophy of 'Zen and the Art of Not Giving a Darn'.

strategic management

Thinking about having someone else somehow doing something sometime.

strategic planning

Thinking about somehow doing something sometime.

strategy

What we're doing next week.

(*See* **tactics**)

streamline

Fishing for efficiency.

strengths

Qualities managers own up to.

stress

1. Quasi-medical condition used to avoid work

2. Overstressed feature of managerial life, but only in the sense that managers impose it on others; the absence of which in humans is found only in cemeteries.

strike

When workers prove their worth by not working.

structure

The concept of diverging and converging and diverging parallel lines connecting the interfaces of the vertices of the dovetailing of the nexus of the organisation's scaffolding.

subcommittee

An uncommitted subgroup of a committee whose role it is to act like a committee until it becomes one.

subordinate

Someone lower than you in the hierarchy, who you are happy to remind of this fact.

success

Failing a course in organisational behaviour.

succession plan

Will.

suggestion box

1. Recycling bin
2. Safety valve for disgruntled employees

3. Safe deposit box

4. Lost property storage.

suicide

A goal pursued by half the human race. The other half pursue homicide. The rest are to decide on deicide.

superego

A very big ego.

supervisor

A very little ego.

support activities

Bottomless pit of demand for resources, often best left underfunded.

suppression

Choosing to repress.

surplus

An accidental profit hidden from government.

survey

A research tool demonstrably invalidated by asking people what they want instead of what they do.

sustainability

Ability to exploit in the future.

sweetener

1. An engagement ring in a marriage proposal

2. A wedding ring in a divorce settlement.

Swiss cheese

The management metaphor alluding to many small failures lining up to cause a catastrophe. Turning a big block of Swiss cheese will sometimes reveal a series of interconnected hollows all the way through.

(*See* '**all your ducks are in a row**')

SWOT analysis

Key strategic planning session tool, illegibly handwritten in multi-colours on butchers' paper. Emphasises strengths, weaknesses, opportunities and threats as the road to the Holy Grail, without which there's nothing to do but adjourn to the bar.

synergy

1. $2 + 2 = 5$

2. Marketing + finance = operations

3. Organisation A + Organisation B = you lose your job

4. Venture capitalists + mergers and acquisitions (M&A) lawyers + firms with which they have no relationship = gross profit for venture capitalists + net profit for M&A lawyers

5. Coal + solar = wind.

system

Something with inputs, throughputs, transformations and outputs, the outcome from which should add value to the organisation.

systems thinking

Not so much the circuitous, annular, radial or circumlocutory process of creating a thinking system as a cyclic practice.

tactics

What we're doing tomorrow.

(*See* **strategy**)

tangible asset

Something valued because of an expected intangible benefit beyond its ephemeral tangibility.

target market

Market.

task completion syndrome

Imperfectionism.

task force

A committee that gets things done.

task-orientated

Facing the task.

task-oriented

Facing the East.

taste

Lip-service to culture.

tautology

Repeating the same thing twice.

tax accounting

That set of accounts which shows the smallest possible profit, and preferably a loss. There are completely different sets of accounts to show your staff, your partners and yourself – the latter including any untraceable cash receipts.

taxation

Differs from other theft only insofar as it is generally misunderstood to be just.

team player

Person lacking initiative.

temperature of an organisation

Cheeky medical metaphor measuring managerial anal-retentiveness, manifested as the manager's belief that he is a thermostat rather than a thermometer.

(*See* **cranial-rectal extraction** *and* **climate**)

temptation

Manage us not into temperance.

test market

Market.

testamur

Written proof that you've wasted your time seeking institutional approval from a college or university, or from society, when you could have been seeking approval from a real live person, for money.

Theory X

Employees are lazy.

Theory Y

No they're not.

thinking

Talking to a better class of person.

thou shalt not

Serious sanctions-supported suggestions.

threats

Indirect incentives.

thrift

1. Drinking Australian champagne
2. Naming it so.

throughput

1. Transformation, often on a transcendental level

2. What you put through something

3. The process between input and output

4. What actually happens in the process of creating a service or product. Senior managers do not know how things are manufactured or created, so this useful wastepaper basket word can be applied to make them look knowledgeable.

time

Either a denominator or a numerator, depending on where you did your math. Or in a pluralistic society, maths.

time and motion study

A method to test whether employees move intertemporally.

time in lieu

The organisational cost of irritable bowel syndrome, brought on by indigestible management decisions.

time management

Management.

Times New Roman

This is a formal font enhanced by curly bits and is the style of choice for snail mail. When it is crucial to say things that can be retracted, Times New Roman is your tool.

to-do list

Something else to remember.

tolerance

Absence of principle (except for that one), which knows no limit (except for that).

totalitarian

Holistic manager.

toxic managers

A waste of office space.

TQM (Total Quality Management)

Continuous self-flagellation.

traction

A word used to describe the uptake of ideas, as in 'Getting traction leads to action'. Similar to 'Hitting the ground running'.

trade association (*also* **industry association**)

A group of employers claiming special needs over those dictated by the marketplace.

trade unionists (*also* **labor unionists**)

1. Economic illiterates who falsely believe that they can increase wages they don't pay by advocating the punishment of those who wish to accept deals the union does not endorse

2. A group sensitive to criticism.

tradition

Dancing with the dead.

trainee

Chairman of the Board.

training

Education that has a purpose.

trance

State induced by attending an AGM.

transference

Psychiatrists telling clients they are mad.

transformation

The belief that you are not yourself but that you will be one day.

transitioning

A person, service or product on the way out.

transparency

1. Accountability adopted after the PR budget is spent

2. A management philosophy to see through

3. Something that you can read from while maintaining eye contact with the audience.

trend analysis

Codifying the past; fashionable tool for measuring how quickly history will continue to set theory.

tried and tested

Wearing a tie.

trust

1. Management naivety

2. Management naiveté.

truth

A debased concept that used to mean 'in accordance with the facts', but now means 'it works for me'. In management, subordinated to power.

turnover

Because it's best that you don't see it.

Type A managers

1. Taiwanese capital executives

2. Cause themselves heart-attacks.

Type B managers

B-grade managers who spend all day alphabetising their tasks.

type C managers

1. Cause heart-attacks in others
2. Create growth – in themselves.

unconscious

That which is unknowable but psychoanalysts assume and managers fall into. Final resting place of the conscience.

undent

To move to the left what had been moved to the right.

(*See the* **Liberal Party of Australia** *and the* **Australian Labor Party**)

underling

1. A New Age person
2. A bed of couscous at a pesco-vegetarian restaurant.

undesirables

Principled board members.

unity of command

A claim that all the organisation's leaders have the same values, vision and mission, and that they are familiar with the latest justifications for implementing any necessary draconian measures.

unity of purpose

1. Fire!
2. Micro-business.

universal

Something that applies equally to everyone and everything – like management theory, McDonald's and democracy.

university of life

1. Cultivated ignorance
2. If you graduate from the university of life, you die
3. Graduate from the school of hard knocks
4. Excuse for having failed high school
5. A person qualified by a degree of chip-on-the-shoulder.

unskilled workers

Managers with pre-career MBAs.

upmarket

A position attractive to brand-conscious consumers.

user-friendly

Self-explanatory.

utilitarianism

The theory that goodness is good.

utility

A really small unit of measure, so tiny that even the concepts of management theory can be quantified using it.

utopia

Workplace without managers.

value judgement

1. A good thing

2. Good in some situations

3. They exist, for better or for worse, and sometimes for neither

4. A bad thing – science must be value-free.

values

Something to fall back on when the cash flow doesn't.

variable costs

Expenditure items that you can't do a darn thing about, but at least you can get them off the balance sheet.

veil of ignorance

Deaf ear, blind eye, transparent résumé.

venture capital

1. Capital you'd almost venture to use if it were your own

2. Money you don't need to return.

vertical integration

Popular among firms with CEOs who are control freaks – such as former CFOs – who like owning all elements of the production and distribution chain, irrespective of profitability.

very good

A balanced scorecard in search of excellent.

vice versa

Verse a vice.

virtual knowledge

Knowing knowledge and ideas related thereto.

virtuous organisation

Good and service replacing goods and services.

vision

1. Something that the CEO has at a management retreat, after too much alcohol and caffeine, followed by too little sleep

2. A representation of how the organisation would look without debt, cash flow challenges or shareholders to report to

3. A perfect response when you don't understand the detail of a problem: 'Is this congruent with our vision?'

4. The management retreat at a beautiful resort, number two in the sequence: values, vision, mission. Don't forget to bring butcher's paper, whiteboard, permanent markers and a slides program to fight over.

wage or wages

Payment dispensed to dispensable employees. The plural makes it seem like more money.

wait

Time between milestones.

walking the talk

Tap-dancing and fire-walking with the masses.

war

1. Destructive crater of management metaphors

2. Failed crisis management

3. Successful issues management.

warehouse

Palatable location for placing over-ordered stock in orderly lines.

watch

Used for measuring the economic worth of an MBA subject.

way forward, the

Useful to employ when asked about plans for the future, as it gives you time to think of an answer.

weaknesses

Always denied by mentioning strengths.

wealth

A financial state rarely felt by the wealthy, as the human appetite for security is insatiable.

weasel words

Words deliberately designed to avoid meaning or commitment: the impactful behaviour of demystifying cultural embedment.

website

(Currently under construction. Please bookmark this page and visit us again soon)

what works

Thinking that feelings are more important than thoughts.

whistle-blower

1. Someone who publicly announces his retirement

2. An intermediary about to be disintermediated

3. Referee

4. Umpire

5. Arbiter

6. Judge

7. Adjudicator

8. Mediator

9. Conciliator

10. High priest

11. Moraliser

12. Prophet

13. Angel

14. God.

(*See* **martyr**)

white-collar

The uniform of the clerical class, worn so that they will not inadvertently be required to do useful work, which would be embarrassing all round.

white-collar crime

1. Crime that pays

2. Getting away with it

3. Not getting away with it.

winners

White-collar criminals.

win-win

One of the quadrants of a particularly useful negotiation theory matrix. The others are:

- win-lose
- lose-win, and
- lose-lose.

wisdom

Rational self-interest, which, if enacted, would eliminate war, religion and management.

wit

1. Someone who says that management is a joke
2. Someone who understands the joke
3. Someone who forgives the joke
4. Someone who shares the joke
5. Management *(adjective)* jokes *(noun)*
6. Management *(noun)* jokes *(verb)*.

witless

(*See* **wit**)

witness

Also known as a fool, because his testimony will be discounted.

work

Something managers get done through other people.

work experience

1. Anthropology for the young
2. Sociology for the youngish
3. Psychology for the young at heart
4. Zoology for the not-so-young.

workaholic

Successful senior executive with a chauffeur, driven to work.

workaphile

A workplace romance without a partner.

work-life balance

A see-sawing, pendulous arc of a continuum, always as wrong as it is right.

world class

We've been on the internet and have copied the very best.

world first

As far as we can tell, if you buy this, you'll be going where no one has gone before.

wrong-clicking

Clicking the right-hand button on a computer mouse, or the right button on a notebook computer touchpad, which reveals uncertainties. Also known as right-clicking.

WTO

World Trade Organisation; not Well Thought Of.

www (wise weasel words)

A random compilation of malicious gossip and unsubstantiated anecdotes, as useful as a clock to a pig.

ex-spouse

Someone who would correct your spelling and alphabetisation when you are out of line. Or alignment.

young

Those who undermine the old.

youth

A growing market.

penultimate

1. One after the antepenultimate

2. Two after the preantepenultimate

3. This

4. Given that there are a range of options and opportunities and possibilities to discuss just before the final point, it would seem to us – and this is something from which we, the authors, would find it hard, if not impossible, to resile – that, at this point in time, in the development of management language, there is a need to set clear boundaries and say, 'This far, and no further'. But maybe just one last thing.

zero-based budgeting

Budgeting for zeros.

INDEX

This book is a dictionary.

But it may help to have the alphabet handy: a b c d e f g h i j k l m n o p q r s t u v w x y z.

Conclusions

Like words and phrases, these are hard to define.

Recommendations

1. Look both ways before you cross the road.

2. Invest in gold.

3. Group things in threes.

Technical terms

1. 'See' means 'see'.

2. 'Compare with' means 'compare with'.

3. 1, 2, 3 and so on mean that each definition is separate.

4. a, b, c and so on mean that each element is part of the larger definition.

5. If V1 is for vision, V2 is for values, M is for mission, S is for strategy, and O is for the organisation, then: $\{[(V1+V2) - M] \times S\} \times O = $ Management.

6. If the cost of S is more than the value of O, then no amount of M will do.

Editorial committee

Affirmative action: Marietta Mann

Agriculture: Sandy Playnz, Beau Vine

Astronomy: Buck McCluster

Aviation: Aaron Orticle

Chemistry: Dan Gerus

Comedy theory: Hugh Moore

Corporate governance: Haydn de Mudd, Rudy Koulis, Perry Pheral

Economics: I.T. de Pendes

Electrical engineering: Anton de Mitteran

Finance: Rhet Eyerment, Seymour Mahoney, Adam Marp

Food technology: André Mayne de Zërt

Futurist studies: Thom Morrow

Gaming: Jacques Podt

Genealogy: Charlie Sarnt, Bob Zyrunkl

Government: Beau Rocraci

Holistic research: Jan Ited

Hospitality: Rob de Geste, Alf Resco

Housing: Mort Gauge, Ulysses Voyd

Information Technology: Artur Pfischel

International affairs: Haydn Zich

Knowledge management: Noel Hedge

Leadership: Mike Bleave, Harry Diculus, Dick Tait

Legal studies: Laura Byding

Logistics: Frank de Poeste

Management: Lou Dicrus, Lou Natick, Lulu

Further reading

Recommended.

Font

The Generic typeface used in this volume is the work of Fontov Wisdom, the noted Eastern European fine artist, radical calligrapher and thief. The Generic font is based on the classical English alphabet prior to before the introduction of vowels being introduced in 1066. It is strongly influenced by the painterly style of pre-Raphaelite public transport graffitists, whereby each letter flows to the other, and each word connects fluidly with the sentence structure. The decisive clarity is reminiscent of the Mauritius dodo quill that Wisdom used in his famous mural inside the Moscow *pissoir*.

Printed in Australia
AUOC02n1539190917
289699AU00003B/4/P